Revolutionary Horizons

Revolutionary Horizons:
Past and Present in Bolivian Politics

FORREST HYLTON
AND SINCLAIR THOMSON

with a Prologue by Adolfo Gilly

VERSO

London • New York

With love for Lina and Steele
and for Seemin and Russell

First published by Verso 2007
© Forrest Hylton and Sinclair Thomson 2007
Epilogue © Adolfo Gilly 2007

The moral rights of the authors have been asserted

1 3 5 7 9 10 8 6 4 2

Verso
UK: 6 Meard Street, London W1F 0EG
USA: 180 Varick Street, New York, NY 10014-4606
www.versobooks.com

Verso is the imprint of New Left Books

ISBN: 978-1-84467-097-0 (pbk)
ISBN: 978-1-84467-070-3 (hbk)

British Library Cataloguing in Publication Data
A catalogue record for this book is available from the British Library

Library of Congress Cataloging-in-Publication Data
A catalog record for this book is available from the Library of Congress

Typeset in AGaramond by Hewer Text UK Ltd, Edinburgh
Printed in the USA by Maple Vail

Contents

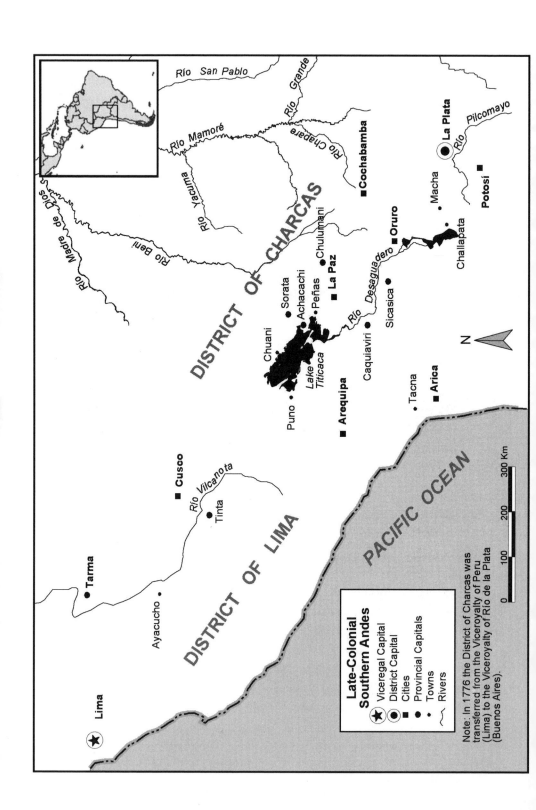

Late-Colonial Southern Andes

★	Viceregal Capital
◉	District Capital
■	Cities
●	Provincial Capitals
•	Towns
⌇	Rivers

Note: In 1776 the District of Charcas was transferred from the Viceroyalty of Peru (Lima) to the Viceroyalty of Río de la Plata (Buenos Aires).

DISTRICT OF CHARCAS

DISTRICT OF LIMA

PACIFIC OCEAN

N

Río San Pablo

Río Grande

Río Mamoré

Río Chapare

Río Yacuma

Río Beni

Río Madre de Dios

Río Pilcomayo

Río Desaguadero

Río Vilcanota

La Plata

Cochabamba

Potosí

Macha

Oruro

Challapata

Chulumani

La Paz

Sorata

Achacachi

Peñas

Chuani

Sicasica

Caquiaviri

Puno

Lake Titicaca

Arequipa

Tacna

Arica

Cusco

Tinta

Tarma

Ayacucho

Lima

0   100   200   300 Km

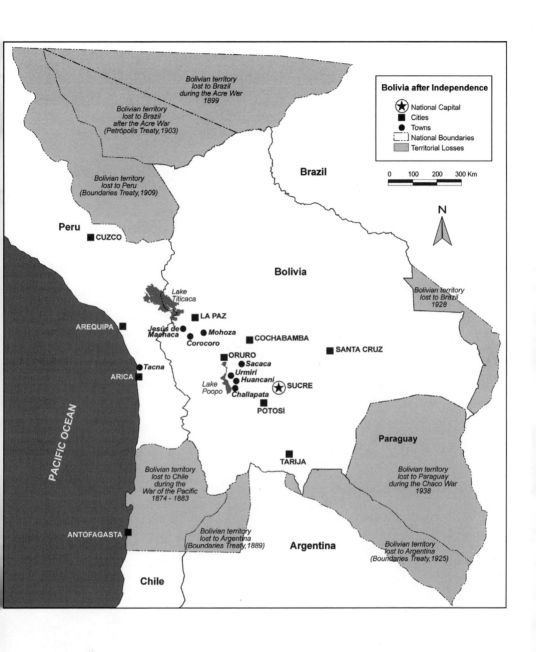

Bolivia after Independence

- ⭐ National Capital
- ■ Cities
- ● Towns
- ┈ National Boundaries
- ▨ Territorial Losses

0   100   200   300 Km

N

Brazil

Bolivian territory lost to Brazil during the Acre War 1899

Bolivian territory lost to Brazil after the Acre War (Petrópolis Treaty, 1903)

Bolivian territory lost to Peru (Boundaries Treaty, 1909)

Peru

■ CUZCO

Bolivia

Lake Titicaca

Bolivian territory lost to Brazil 1928

■ LA PAZ

■ AREQUIPA

● Jesús de Machaca   ● Mohoza

Corocoro

■ COCHABAMBA

■ SANTA CRUZ

● Tacna

■ ARICA

● ORURO
● Sacaca
Urmiri
Huancani
⭐ SUCRE

Lake Poopo

Challapata

■ POTOSI

PACIFIC OCEAN

Paraguay

■ TARIJA

Bolivian territory lost to Paraguay during the Chaco War 1938

Bolivian territory lost to Chile during the War of the Pacific 1874 - 1883

■ ANTOFAGASTA

Bolivian territory lost to Argentina (Boundaries Treaty, 1889)

Argentina

Bolivian territory lost to Argentina (Boundaries Treaty, 1925)

Chile

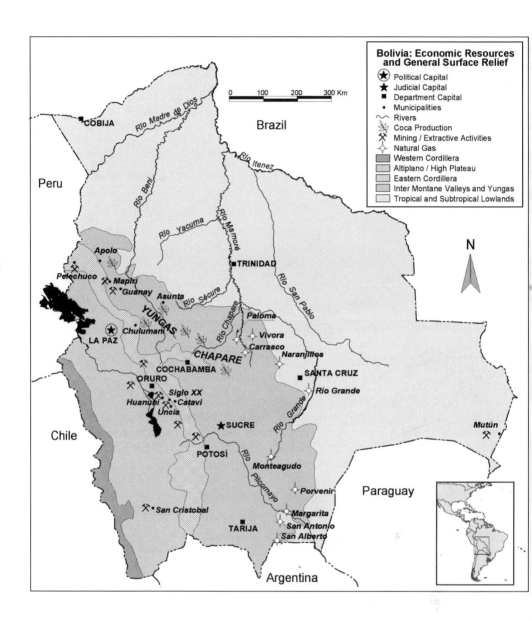

Bolivia: Economic Resources and General Surface Relief

"I will return as millions."

Attributed to Tupaj Katari, 1781

"It is not enough to have taken away Toussaint. There are 2,000 leaders to be taken away."

Gen. Charles Leclerc to Napoleon Bonaparte, Saint-Domingue, 1802

✳ "It's very hard for you all to understand because you have been taught the exact opposite every day, on television and in the press, and hence you lose sight of the fact of the people down below and what the people down below are capable of doing."

C.L.R. James, on the Haitian Revolution, 1971

"Men fight and lose the battle, and the thing that they fought for comes about in spite of defeat, and when it comes it turns out not to be what they meant, and other men have to fight for what they meant under another name."

William Morris, 1886

Indian Peasant March, May 2005. © Noah Friedman-Rudovsky

Prologue:

The Spirit of Revolt

In Bolivia in mid-October 2003, a popular insurrection had been going on for days in El Alto, a city of 800,000 workers, peasants, migrants, and petty merchants, most of them indigenous. Four hundred meters below, insurrectionary *alteños* [residents of El Alto] controlled the gateway to La Paz and blocked the supply of fuel to the capital of the republic. Surrounded, the government decided to break the blockade with a military convoy that opened a path up to the city by firing on, and killing, dozens of people. This is how it cleared the way for trucks loaded with gas cisterns to get down to the capital.

Alteños collected their dead, held wakes in their churches and homes, and said, "Enough!" With the strength of men and women, young and old, they pulled train cars along the tracks from the station and pushed them off a bridge, so that many meters below, the cars blocked the highway leading from La Paz to El Alto—the very route by which the truckloads of soldiers had come to make way for the gas cisterns. "Enough! No one else gets through here!"

The following day, they started to descend, by the dozens or perhaps even hundreds of thousands, to occupy the city of La Paz, while from the other side of the valley, more unending columns of Indians ascended, with the same goal: to take the capital and overthrow the murderous creole regime of Gonzalo Sánchez de Lozada. By then, the middle class in La Paz supported El Alto and demanded a government ceasefire. The army did not dare to keep killing. The government fell, and Gonzalo Sánchez de Lozada fled to the United States.

The history of this fraction of time that explodes out of quotidian time as a sort of shift in destiny; the history of this instantaneous time called revolution, its past, its ancestors, its protagonists, their reasoning and motives, is the subject of this book by Forrest Hylton and Sinclair Thomson. They were there, and have spent years studying Bolivia's indigenous revolts and revolutions.

A classic revolution, at the very beginning of the twenty-first century, has taken place in Bolivia, a cycle of popular rebellion that began with the "Water War" in 2000 and culminated in the indigenous insurrections of 2003 and 2005, which twice seized the capital, and forced early elections in December 2005. With an absolute majority, and for the first time in Bolivian history, an Indian leader became president of the republic.

This book boldly and rightly affirms that what happened was a revolution, and demonstrates it through history, analysis, and chronicle. A revolution, that which no longer existed, a violent and liberating revolution like all others in history: here it was again, bringing back the spirit of revolt out of grievance and out of the past.

After chronicling the cycle of popular mobilization since 2000 that led to such an outcome, Hylton and Thomson seek out its roots, premonitions, and precursors in the long time-spans of history. Bolivia is an Indian country, a place where two-thirds of the population recognizes and declares itself to be Aymara, Quechua, Guaraní, or of other indigenous groups governed since Spanish conquest by a white and *mestizo* minority. Since the sixteenth century, the relationship between rulers and ruled, and between dominant and subaltern groups, has had a specific feature, indelible as skin color. As in the rest of the colonial universe born in that century, the relationship took the form of racial subordination.

The first great indigenous insurrection against this domination—which preceded the Wars of Independence—was led by Tupaj Katari in 1781. Indian armies imposed a prolonged blockade of La Paz, which was only broken with the arrival of troops from the distant city of Buenos Aires, capital of the Viceroyalty of Río de la Plata.

Defeat did not erase the memory for indigenous people, who have known ever since that they once laid siege to the city of the "*señores*," nor for the white and *mestizo* minority, as successive generations have transmitted until today the fear—denied, but always living on at the threshold of consciousness—of a new siege on the city by a limitless dark-skinned population.

In April 1952, a popular insurrection exploded in defense of a presidential election stolen by the dominant oligarchy. Known as the "April Revolution," rebels took the city of La Paz, dispersed the army, overthrew the president, established a *mestizo* government that nationalized the mines—the principal Bolivian industry—decreed an agrarian reform, and had to live for years with the parallel power of miners', workers', and peasants' unions, their armed militias, and community radio stations. Of course, miners, workers, and peasants were Indians, and their indigenous languages were used to debate in their assemblies and to communicate during their celebrations and in their homes.

After a long period of vicissitudes and tenacious resistance, beginning in the 1980s the new power of the neoliberal world reorganized Bolivia, closed the mines, dismantled trade unions, and dispersed workers and their settlements. The April Revolution was no more than a historical reference. Order was re-established. Once again, Indians were put in their place.

But like all domination with racial roots, nationalist ideology and the shared symbolism between dominant and subaltern groups was merely a thin, formal layer, and hegemony a fractured and fragile covering. Under-neath lived the persistent and vast human community of the indigenous, those life-worlds that filmmaker Jorge Sanjinés called "The Clandestine Nation." Since Tupaj Katari, and even before, those worlds never ceased to emerge, here and there, to break up the surface of domination with violent local revolts that were rapidly put down and punished, but not forgotten.

This nation, negated by the liberal republic, was also nearly invisible for the republican left, which confused it with Indian positions in economy and society: peasants, factory workers, miners, petty merchants, artisans. The republican left did not, therefore, see the ancient place that this nation occupied in the colonial world and that persisted in the republic: Indians, people the color of the earth; Aymaras, Quechuas, Guaraníes, Urus, those who, on the shores of Lake Titicaca, claim to be the most ancient of human beings.

Each time the country today called Bolivia begins to move, the clan-destine nation reappears, or better, makes itself violently visible and audi-ble, as Edward P. Thompson put it, taking leading places on the stage previously occupied by noisy politicians, bureaucrats, military men, investors, and their scribes.

That is how it made itself present in October 2003 when people descended on La Paz and took it over, unfurling their flags and symbols and putting forth their bodies, and their dead, as Thomson and Hylton note: "Beginning with Warisata in September, and spreading to El Alto in October, the mourning of martyrs provided a time to express grief and fury, to bolster the spirit through ritual and reflection, and to dedicate ongoing struggle to those who had lost their lives. The martyrs also provided a new example of indigenous patriotism in Bolivia, insofar as Aymaras were the ones defending the nation against foreign control."

Revolutionary Horizons speaks to us of continuities and ruptures in time, of the cruelty and fragility of internal colonial domination, of centuries-old dispossession and impious exploitation; of the immaterial inheritance of memories and experiences; of how the spirit of revolt has been transmitted across generations through protest, mass clandestinity, and everyday life amidst discrimination and difference. The inheritors and bearers of Andean civilization might well say, "Generations come and generations go, but the earth lasts forever."

The authors put it as follows: "In this book, we approach revolutionary 'horizons' not only as those perspectives of men and women in the past who looked upon the possibilities of future social transformation. For there is another sense of the word. At an archeological site, the phased strata of the earth and the remains of human settlement that are exposed by careful digging are called 'horizons'. We offer this then as an excavation of Andean revolution, whose successive layers of historical sedimentation make up the subsoil, loam, landscape, and vistas for current political struggle in Bolivia."

Thus the revolution of October 2003 and its aftermath in June 2005 are presented as the condensation, in two decisive moments, of the previous experiences of rage, humiliation, and desire: a resounding explosion, an illumination that lights up an instant, a break in the time of everyday life in which linear time, circular time, and messianic time whirl and mix together. This temporal break passes, and does not last, but its resonances and dissonances never die down. They come to be known as years and lives unfold, as Thomson and Hylton tell us at the end of their book.

A victorious revolution, like the Bolivian one in October, implies a deep change in institutions and political leadership, which happened in the presidential elections of December 2005 and the inaugural ceremony of

Indian President Evo Morales in January 2006. Although connected, the new political leadership and the revolution that brought it about are two phenomena that differ in substance.

The new power is a result of the revolution, not its embodiment. In their final reflections, Hylton and Thomson tackle this crucial question. People do not go into a revolution on behalf of an image of the society of the future, Leon Trotsky noted, but because present society has become intolerable. Their revolt nurtures itself on the image of enslaved ancestors, not the ideal of liberated descendants, wrote Walter Benjamin.

A revolution means that nothing goes back to being what it was before in the spirits of the living and their relations with each other. It also pays homage to the dead, rescues the memory and the trials and tribulations of humiliated ancestors, and renovates the symbolic universe. That is why a revolution has repercussions in places and in times yet to come. But its duration is short. And if, when it manages to triumph, a revolution engenders a new political leadership, the insurrection is neither embodied by nor prolonged in it, and the break in time closes: "*mais il est bien court le temps des cerises.*" What then follows concerns a subsequent time, even as the new leadership continues to affirm, "I am the revolution."

It is important to debate and assess the composition and subsequent changes in political leadership that arise out of a revolution. But to subsume its analysis and its meaning in this fashion is to lose one's way and to enter into a shadow play. This is frequently done by those who, without suspecting it, have themselves become shadows of real life, which goes on elsewhere, far from them.

The history of revolutions is usually treated in terms of the consolidation of a new order. In other words, revolution is a necessary prelude to the new order. This is not the way this book considers the third Bolivian revolution, which inaugurated the twenty-first century on the *altiplano.*

Thomson and Hylton concede the importance of the Movement Toward Socialism (MAS), headed by Evo Morales, as a channel and political instrument for the popular insurrection, in which social movements played the leading role. They note, "Morales and MAS tail-ended, rather than led, the insurrection of 2003 and 2005. [But] in the electoral arena, Morales and MAS have served as the only effective vehicle for national articulation of the heterogeneous movements."

Nevertheless, they continue, this does not authorize the leadership to uphold that in the future indigenous sectors do not need representation as Indians (in the Constitutional Assembly, for example), on the grounds that "they have already received representation – through MAS." Instead of continuing to resist, the official argument runs, these sectors "need to locate themselves in this new time of occupying structures of power."

Both historians go against such an argument: "Whatever their intent, such statements de-authorized, marginalized, and silenced indigenous demands. It was a new example of the condescension that has plagued Indian-Left relations historically and that has pushed indigenous activists into more radically autonomous positions." An indigenous president is not enough to turn the clandestine nation into the Republic.

It is necessary, of course, to understand the inelastic limits that those who govern run into, whether it be the ferocious resistance of the classes that have been displaced from power, and their political and economic representatives, foreign as well as domestic; or the steel cage in which the new global neoliberal order encloses possibilities of action, along with the imminent presence of its powerful material base—the Pentagon, the military force of the United States; or the material limits of scarcity, national isolation, and poverty.

In the words of the authors, "There are consequences of the present whose force will be difficult to obstruct or reverse in the near future. And yet, if history has shown that revolutionary moments leave an indelible mark on the future, it has shown that internal colonialism and class hierarchies are durable structures as well."

But for this very reason, the popular movements that gave rise to the new configuration of state power cannot lose themselves in it. They must maintain not indifference or neutrality, but rather their autonomy and independence.

We need to treat the history of revolutions as the history of those unique moments in which the forgotten, the oppressed, the humiliated—those who make the world with their hands, bodies, and minds—rise up and suspend the time of contempt to inaugurate a new time; moments, unforgettable whether long or short, of revelation of their own being, their own intelligence, and their own inheritance, which is that of all human beings.

"Not man or men but the struggling, oppressed class itself is the depository of historical knowledge. In Marx it appears as the last enslaved class, the avenger that completes the task of liberation in the name of generations of the downtrodden," wrote Walter Benjamin in his "Theses on the Philosophy of History." There, the spirit of revolt survives and burns in secret, in diverse times and places.

Those moments in which that spirit comes to light and stirs like gale winds, those breaks in time whose duration should be multiplied by their intensity, can later be suspended and converted into memory and the past. But they also become lived experience and, as a result, ongoing reverberations into all the possible futures of those who lived through those moments as a people.

These are the themes of this exceptional book, which is the work of two historians who have followed and lived Bolivian life. *Revolutionary Horizons* is a chronicle, a history, and an archaeology of indigenous insurgency on the Andean high plains, and, at the same time, a mature fruit of study, experience, and reflection.

Adolfo Gilly
Ciudad de México, 7 May 2007

Preface

The makings of this book go back to the days of October 2003 when we witnessed the insurrection in La Paz and El Alto that overthrew the government of Bolivian President Gonzalo Sánchez de Lozada. As historians of Indian politics and insurgency, it was extraordinary to see a phenomenon we were only used to imagining faintly, through eighteenth- and nineteenth-century archival documents, unfold before our own eyes. And what riveted us were the many remarkable resemblances—beginning with the siege of La Paz itself—between earlier historical experiences and contemporary dynamics. Then in May and June of 2005, we witnessed the power of Indian and popular mobilization again, in an uprising that brought an end to the government of President Carlos Mesa.

As we lived through those times of great political intensity and instability, we sustained an ongoing conversation and began collaborating in an attempt to make sense of what was unfolding in Bolivia and how it related to the country's past. In December 2003, we put out a volume in Spanish—*Ya es otro tiempo el presente: Cuatro momentos de insurgencia indígena*—co-authored with Felix Patzi and Sergio Serulnikov, with a prologue by Adolfo Gilly. Our own conversation was informed by countless others with friends and colleagues in Bolivia, and we were especially fortunate to enter into dialogue with Adolfo Gilly, who was visiting New York University from Mexico in the spring of 2003. Subsequent correspondence with Adolfo, discussions with him in La Paz at the end of that year, and his writings have made a deep impression on our thinking. We shared a few things in common from the start: a preference for a historical vantage point on the present, a commitment to bottom-up approaches to politics, and a passion for Bolivia. But it was Adolfo's own lightning-quick, yet contextualized, understanding of the revolutionary nature of Bolivian events that influenced us most.

We have sought to stimulate another dialogue in our book, a potential dialogue not exactly of our own invention, but one which in our view has been mainly frustrated within Bolivia and utterly ignored outside it. Our intention is to bring together into a single account two different and even partially contradictory strains of historical and political analysis originally developed by intellectuals from Bolivia.

One is the rich heritage of René Zavaleta Mercado, Bolivia's foremost political theorist who came of age in the revolutionary period of the 1950s and who thought critically and creatively up until the time of his death in Mexico in 1984, at the time of the collapse of Bolivia's Democratic Popular Unity (UDP) government. His intellectual trajectory followed a general arc from revolutionary nationalism to a critical and creative Marxism that drew especially from Antonio Gramsci. The full scope of Zavaleta's work is impossible to encapsulate here, yet among his primary concerns were nationalism, state formation, and working-class power. His brilliant but truncated final work, *Lo nacional-popular en Bolivia* (1986), opened up historical inquiry into popular nationalist projects and the self-determination of Indian, plebeian, and proletarian classes. Zavaleta's own agenda here—tracing national-popular struggle in successive epochs of Bolivian history—sets one of the fundamental tracks for our own study.

Zavaleta was always conscious that political struggle in one's own time shapes the epistemological horizon for one's analysis. In his own case, it was the vicissitudes of the national revolution in Bolivia and the strengths and limitations of the country's proletariat in the mid-twentieth century that shaped his theoretical investigations. Yet what Zavaleta largely overlooked was the emergence at the end of his life of another political movement that would come to have major intellectual implications. The rise of an Indian peasant trade union organization in the late 1970s led to new critiques of the enduring forms of colonial and racial-ethnic domination in the country. This *katarista* movement and critical consciousness drew from the Indianist writings of Fausto Reinaga since the 1960s, yet also from left analyses of capitalist exploitation.

Young Aymara professionals, especially historians, sociologists, and pedagogues, cadre in small Indianist political parties, and leaders in the peasant trade unions shared basic perspectives, even if they differed over issues of collaboration with left parties and with mestizo or creole allies. Within *katarista* discourse, which took its name from Tupaj Katari, who led an Aymara army against Spanish colonial forces in 1781, historical consciousness was central. One particularly vibrant nucleus for Indian intellectual production was the Andean Oral History Workshop (THOA), founded in 1983 by students from the Sociology Department in the Universidad Mayor de San Andrés in La Paz. A critical *katarista* text which laid out in incisive terms the history of indigenous struggles in the twentieth century, as well as the power of long-term and short-term political memory in the present, was THOA co-founder Silvia Rivera Cusicanqui's *Oppressed but not Defeated: Peasant Struggles among the Aymara and Qhechwa in Bolivia, 1900–1980* (1987), which originally appeared in Spanish in 1984. This *katarista* project—tracing Indian struggles in southern Andean history—sets the second fundamental track for our own study.

These two tracks of analysis have more often than not followed separate courses, just as creole left and proletarian political projects have diverged from Indian ones since the 1980s, amidst substantial mistrust and miscommunication. We can illustrate their coming together in this book by borrowing metaphorically from a feature of traditional Andean culture: the *tinku*. As we explain in the conclusion, the *tinku* is a ritualized combat, a charged encounter that brings together two distinguishable parts of an Andean community. The parts may exist in sharp tension with one another, but their differences must be confronted in order to redefine the ever-shifting balance of forces within the community, in order to achieve the cyclical renewal of communal health, fertility, and relations with the sacred. *Revolutionary Horizons* represents a sort of *tinku* in history-writing.

As Zavaleta and the recent generation of Aymara historians have recognized, knowledge is produced according to the political conditions that give rise to it. Our own experiences in Bolivia, and especially the powerful events of 2003 and 2005, shaped the conception and purposes of this book. Our effort in what follows is to bring together into a single account the histories of both Indian and national-popular struggles, based on two different intellectual currents that have been produced by those struggles. The power and depth of the transformations in present-day Bolivia, we argue, are the direct result of a historic convergence between these two different traditions of struggle.

The epigraphs point to key dimensions of this history: the power of bottom-up mobilization in revolutionary moments, and of the cyclical dynamics of revolutionary struggle. The quotation attributed to Tupaj Katari comes from the rich subaltern political culture found in Bolivia. The other excerpts reinforce these points while signaling popular and revolutionary struggles further afield, in England and the Caribbean since the late eighteenth century. They also point to two of our historiographic inspirations: the author of *The Black Jacobins*, C.L.R. James, and William Morris's biographer, Edward P. Thompson.

*   *   *

In La Paz and El Alto, we would particularly like to thank Rossana Barragán and the Archivo Histórico de La Paz, Lina Britto, Alejandro Choque, Lucila Choque, Vidal Choque, Colectivo de Mujeres Alteñas, Comuna, Pati Costas, Jean Paul Guevara, Gustavo Guzmán, Indymedia Bolivia/Qollasuyo, Ben Kohl, Tom Kruse, Pablo Mamani, Valentín Mamani, Dunia Mukrani, Oscar Olivera, Johnny Orihuela, Raul Prada, Seemin Qayum, Tania Quiroz, Radio Wayna Tambo, Silvia Rivera Cusicanqui, Gonzalo Rojas, Martín Sivak, Luis Tapia, Esteban Ticona, Oscar Vega, Jorge Viaña, Fabian Yaksic, and Juan de Dios Yapita. Elsewhere, thanks to Aijaz Ahmad, Teo Ballvé and *NACLA Report on the Americas*, Mike Davis, James Dunkerley, Laura Gotkowitz, Brooke Larson, Staughton Lynd, Ng'ethe Maina, Aldo Marchesi, Tom Penn at Verso, Marcus Rediker, Gerardo Renique, José Luis Renique, Gonzalo Sánchez, Irene Tung, Susan Watkins and *New Left Review*, and Jeff Webber.

Special thanks go to Noah Friedman-Rudovsky for his generosity with his photographs, and to Bennett Campoverde for his generous collaboration on the maps. Thanks also to Luis Gómez and Martha Cajías for their creative support.

We were fortunate to have discussed earlier versions of the manuscript at Comuna in La Paz in November 2004, the International Center for Advanced Studies at New York University, and the Culture, Power, Boundaries Seminar at Columbia University in September 2005, and the Coordinadora del Agua in Cochabamba in November 2006.

Yuspajara, tatanaka mamanaka.

PART I

Pachakuti: Andean Transformations

Miners Marching, La Paz, June 2005. © Noah Friedman-Rudovsky

1

The *Plaza* and the *Palacio*

From the mid-1980s through the 1990s, Bolivia stood out as a shining trophy in the global showcase of neoliberalism, as a model for free-market capitalist reforms that international financial institutions urged other "less developed countries" to emulate. In 1985, Bolivia's political class had applied the orthodox economic strictures of the International Monetary Fund to halt inflation, discipline labor, shrink state management of the economy, and open the country to penetration by foreign capital. In the 1990s, it found novel ways to justify the privatization of state industry—especially oil and natural gas production—and the decentralization of state administration with seemingly populist and multicultural reforms.

Throughout much of the twentieth century, Bolivia's trade unions were among the most combative in the world, and grew out of a powerful matrix of peasant community politics dating back to the eighteenth century. By the neoliberal hour of the 1990s, the historic power of working-class and peasant political forces appeared to be decisively broken, as technocratic politicians, working closely with international agencies and the US government, ruled Bolivia with middle-class approval and popular resignation.

By the early twenty-first century, however, Bolivia gained international attention—or notoriety—precisely because of the depth and breadth of popular repudiation of its once vaunted neoliberal order. Beginning in 2000, social movements forcefully rejected the state's abdication of its sovereignty over natural resource wealth, the political corruption and monopoly over decision-making at the national level, and the state's increasing recourse to violence against civilian demonstrators. Despite earlier appearances, the strength and effectiveness of recent protests owe much to the durability of indigenous peasant and working-class political cultures, which provide an extraordinary potential for resistance, symbolic as well as strategic and tactical.

A dramatic wave of mobilizations led to the election of an indigenous president, a phenomenon virtually unheard of in the Western hemisphere, whose agenda responded to the demands of the country's indigenous majority for political representation and national sovereignty over natural resources. The election of a head of state who defended the interests of Andean growers of coca leaf came as an additional blow to the United States, whose policies not only promote neoliberalism but criminalize Andean countries and peoples through a "war on drugs."

The dramatic turnabout in Bolivia has been at the center of heated debates in the Andes, Latin America, and indeed the world. At issue are neoliberalism and its decline, energy resources and their exploitation by transnational corporations, the power of social—and especially indige-nous—movements vis-à-vis the state, Latin America's turn to the left, and the possibilities for social revolution in the contemporary world.

Bolivia's New Era

This turn of events came about through an unusual mix of direct and representative democracy: the action of autonomous social movements as well as unforeseen electoral developments in local, regional, and national politics. The expansion of popular sovereignty in Bolivia—understood as self-government by the majority—began at the municipal level in Cochabamba on 4–12 April 2000, in an effort to block the privatization of water. This was a project backed by the World Bank, and a multinational consortium dominated by the Bechtel Corporation won the contract (there were no other bids) to supply the city's water. During these fervent "Days of April," popular meetings contained various levels of participation, Oscar Olivera relates: "The workers came together in small assemblies according to sector—all of the irrigation farmers [*regantes*], for example, or the business men, or the factory workers." Against the restricted, exclusionary democracy of technocratic neoliberal rule, "a space was created." Here, "people could participate in the political process by discussing the issues and trying to reach a consensus about what the next step should be."[1] In Cochabamba, "the people" (*el pueblo*) reclaimed natural resources for the region, defended use rights against property rights, expelled a multinational water consortium sanctioned by the Bolivian government and international financial institutions, and called for a constitutional assembly that would draft a new charter for political representation. They thus envisioned an end to the *partidocracia*—the system of governing pacts by which traditional political parties managed the neoliberal model. Popular forces overwhelmed police and soldiers through non-violent mobilization to convert Cochabamba's public *plazas* into platforms for democratic assembly and decision-making.

The victory in Cochabamba was succeeded by waves of Indian and peasant insurgency in the western highlands of La Paz and Oruro, in the southwestern highland valleys of Chuquisaca and Potosí, and in the tropical Chapare lowlands northeast of Cochabamba itself. Between April 2000 and September 2003, the snarling tactics of marches, road blockades in the provinces, and urban siege crippled state authority. Traditional party delegates to congress turned a deaf ear to popular demands, while government officials negotiated in bad faith or simply dispatched troops to resolve the conflict. State legitimacy crumbled as the toll in lives surpassed several hundred, and public disaffection mounted.

In October 2003, Aymara Indian communities in the Andean highlands and urban Aymaras from the adjoining cities of El Alto and La Paz spear-headed a successful effort, eventually national in scope, to overthrow the most representative figure of the neoliberal right in Bolivia. Gonzalo Sánchez de Lozada, known to Bolivians as "Goni," had abrogated Bolivian sovereignty over oil and natural gas two days before the end of his first term as President in 1997, offering up these sought-after hydrocarbon resources to transnational energy corporations in exchange for minimal royalties. He then tried to seal an export deal behind closed doors during his second term, which began in August 2002. When he responded to the massive protests in 2003 not only with accusations of subversion but with tanks and open gunfire, Sánchez de Lozada triggered a fierce popular insurrection. Even progressives from middle- and upper-middle-class neighborhoods in La Paz launched hunger strikes and took to the streets and airwaves in the last few days of the insurrection to demand the president's resignation. On 17 October, Sánchez de Lozada boarded a plane to Miami and Vice-President Carlos Mesa—journalist, official historian, and media mogul—assumed power. The insurrection thus meant an embarrassing setback for the US Embassy, which had earlier declared its unwillingness to recognize a new, transitional regime produced by popular power and protest. It was a stunning blow to the "Washington Consensus" that brought neoliberal regimes to power in Latin America in the 1980s and 1990s.

There followed an anguished two-year stalemate in which the governments of former Vice-President Carlos Mesa and former head of the Supreme Court Eduardo Rodríguez Veltzé occupied the empty shell of executive office. Both were isolated constitutional successors rather than elected officials backed by a party apparatus. The social movements nucleated in the highlands and valleys held effective power, and were accompanied in congress by representatives of Evo Morales's Movement to Socialism (MAS) party. They had brought about the collapse of the traditional parties, determined who assumed executive authority, and cornered the legislature. Yet they were unable to enforce fulfillment of the popular mandate when Mesa recoiled from his initial promises to meet their demands. Meanwhile, retreating conservative elites regrouped in the south and east around the regionalist civic committees, especially in lowland Santa Cruz. The fate of the country's rich natural gas reserves still topped the political agenda. Popular movements in the highlands and valleys called for renationalization of the energy sector, to allow the state greater control over resource exploitation and to enable redistribution of revenues to the popular majority. In the opposing camp, the regionalist rulers of the eastern lowlands rejected central government controls and asserted autonomous rights to the resources found within the territory of their departments.[2]

This impasse was finally swept away with the overwhelming victory of Evo Morales in the national elections of December 2005 and his jubilant inauguration in January 2006. His young party (MAS) had made a rapid and dizzying ascent, and was poised to fill the vacuum of state power. It also received a mandate set by the social movements from whose ranks MAS had emerged. A political party that had grown up in the coca fields of the Chapare lowlands and the peasant trade union halls of nearby Cochabamba now stepped—at once incredulous, wary, and brash—into the chambers of the national palace.

Over the first six months of its term, as international onlookers watched intently, the new government responded to the popular mandate with remarkable efficiency. It issued a formal convocation for a constitutional assembly that would "re-found" the Bolivian nation. It decreed the "nationalization" of the country's coveted hydrocarbon resources. It announced an agrarian "revolution" that would redistribute no less than 20 million hectares—nearly a fifth of the country's arable lands—over five years. In August 2006, after another national election of delegates, the constitutional assembly convened in the city of Sucre—the country's judicial capital in the temperate southwestern valley region—to begin the process of drafting a new national charter. This had been precisely the demand of activists and grassroots community forces in Cochabamba in April of 2000, though they had no way of knowing it would come to pass so soon, nor what the consequences would be.

Historical and Regional Perspective

An exceptional historical phase in its own right, this process unfolded as it did because of previous historical cycles dating back over decades and centuries in the territory today known as Bolivia. As events unfolded between 2000 and 2006, history also provided a set of signs and scripts by which the protagonists understood their world, their actions, and their aims. This book inquires into these layers of causality and memory. It offers a historical lens to bring the contemporary cycle into focus and extend our political depth of field.

Our overriding purpose, then, is to demonstrate that a historical perspective is essential for understanding contemporary Bolivian politics. Recent and dramatic transformations in the country have come about through the convergence of two traditions of political struggle—an Indian tradition and what, following Bolivian political theorist René Zavaleta Mercado, we call a "national-popular" tradition. We also argue that the present is a revolutionary moment, the third great social revolution in the land called "Bolivia." The Indian tradition of political struggle can be traced back to 1780–81 when anti-colonial revolution led by Tupaj Amaru, Tupaj Katari, and Tomás Katari challenged Spanish domination in the southern Andes. The "national-popular" tradition culminated in 1952–53 when working-class, peasant, and progressive middle-class forces overthrew an oligarchic order established after Bolivian independence in 1825.

Bolivia's current revolutionary moment may seem the latest in a series of regional challenges to neoliberalism in South America that began with the overthrow of Abdalá Bucaram in Ecuador in May 1997, the election of Hugo Chávez in Venezuela in November 1998, the overthrow of Jamil Mahuad in January 2000, again in Ecuador, the fall of Alberto Fujimori in Peru in November 2000, the overthrow of Fernando de la Rúa in Argentina in December 2001, and the overthrow of Lucio Gutiérrez in (yet again) Ecuador in April 2005. In all five countries, traditional parties that implemented the "Washington Consensus" are in terminal crisis, and mass movements of protest have hastened their downfall.

While Bolivia partly conforms to an emerging regional political pattern, there are important distinctions between countries, especially in the relationship between popular power and state power.[3] Ecuador resembles Bolivia in having produced a powerful indigenous movement, headed by the Confederation of Indigenous Nationalities of Ecuador (CONAIE), yet popular forces in the country have had difficulty controlling state authorities and setting the agenda for national policy, though this might change if newly-elected President Rafael Correa succeeds in convening a constitutional assembly in line with popular demands (inspired, in part, by Bolivian example). Argentina likewise saw the emergence of an effervescent popular movement, joining neighborhood and *piquetero* (unemployed worker) activists, yet it was unable to sustain its momentum and exercise ongoing influence over the political elite. In Venezuela, political transformation has occurred at the level of the state and then worked from the top down to channel the existing energies of grassroots organizations, chiefly in the vast barrios of Caracas. In Bolivia, by contrast, impressive popular power has flowed from the bottom up, setting the parameters for national political and economic debate and putting in place authorities at the national as well as regional and local levels. In no other Latin American country have popular forces achieved so much through their own initiative.

Also, despite apparent parallels in neighboring countries, we should avoid treating crisis and change in Bolivia simply as local effects of a predictable transnational phenomenon. We should not take "neoliberalism" or "globalization" to be an autonomous agent that restructures local societies and inevitably generates its own opposition and collapse, nor should we assume that mass uprisings form a single wave inevitably sweeping from country to country. Rather, our understanding must come first from within, by looking at the grounded local processes of Bolivian history.

The Days of October

On 17 October 2003, dense crowds snaked their way through downtown thoroughfares to take over the Plaza San Francisco in the heart of La Paz, political capital of the Bolivian republic. The marchers were members of popular neighborhood associations from El Alto, a city of more than 800,000 situated 4,000 meters above sea level on the upper rim of La Paz, in which 74 percent claim indigenous Aymara identity; members of the heavily Aymara hillside neighborhood associations of Munaypata, Villa Victoria, and Villa Fátima; market women belonging to urban guild associations; students and unemployed youth; mine workers from Huanuni, an enclave south of the city of Oruro; coca growers and peasant settlers from the subtropical Yungas valleys northeast of La Paz; and members of Aymara peasant communities from the high plateau, led by the insurgent district of Achacachi. Their numbers ranged between 250,000 and 500,000, making this Bolivia's largest demonstration since October 1982, when opposition forces ended the long period of military dictatorship (1964–1982), inaugurated the era of representative democracy, and brought the Democratic Popular Unity (UDP), a center-left coalition government, to power.

This was unlike earlier crowds, however. In 1982, left political parties and the still robust Bolivian Workers' Central (COB) had organized the demonstrations expressing progressive "national-popular" forces that united middle-class dissidents, including students, intellectuals, and professionals, along with workers from urban and mining centers and peasants. In 2003, neither the opposition parties nor the trade unions headed the multitudinous assembly or provided comparable political representation during the uprising that had led to it. The turnout of progressive students, intellectuals, and professionals from the mestizo and creole middle classes was low, while the ranks of urban and rural laborers of Aymara descent swelled downtown streets.[4]

The distinguishing features of the massive urban protest on 17 October— the self-organization of those who took over the capital and their largely indigenous profile—reflected the overall insurrectionary dynamic that brought about the downfall of President Sánchez de Lozada that same day. In important respects, this was a leaderless Aymara uprising rooted in a history of communal Indian struggle dating back over two centuries to the time of the great Andean revolution of 1780–1. Yet despite the differences between 1982 and 2003, there were also important resemblances between the "Days of October" and previous popular uprisings and revolutionary processes in modern Bolivian history.

In earlier experiences of "national-popular" struggle, a heterogeneous array of social groups, with the organized working class foremost among them, joined together to demand democratic transformation of internal relations between state and society, thereby reconstituting political and economic spheres within the country, as well as renegotiating external relations with other states and foreign capital.[5] Such a process took place during the national revolution of 1952 and was underway again in the late 1970s and early 1980s, and there are important points of coincidence today. Rural peasant and urban workers from a range of formal and informal occupations mobilized simultaneously and were ultimately supported by progressive middle-class fractions.[6] They shared a central agenda of sweeping away an unrepresentative and repressive political regime, establishing sovereign control over national resources, and convoking a constitutional assembly to restructure national political and economic life. Over the course of the political conflict in October, the articulation of a new "national-popular" bloc with a coherent set of demands took shape.

Generally, Indian and national-popular struggles in Bolivia have followed separate historical paths, and misapprehension, suspicion, and manipulation have plagued the relations between Indian and progressive mestizo or creole political leaders and intellectuals. It is not that Indian elements have been entirely absent in national-popular struggles, or that national elements are necessarily absent in Indian struggles. Nonetheless, what has tended to prevail is disarticulation, dissonance, or *desencuentro*. When present, Indian elements have been subordinated in national-popular blocs; and, when present, Indian conceptions of nationality (whether notions of the compatibility between being Indian and being Bolivian, or of rights to autonomy or self-determination) have conflicted with "progressive" mestizo and creole conceptions, which cast Indians as archaic survivals from the remote past who need to be modernized.

The infrequent moments of convergence between these traditions, however, have received little scholarly attention, even though they bred powerful radical movements and left lasting effects. The October insurrection—combining elements of past Indian and national-popular struggles in novel ways—stands out historically as one of these exceptional moments of convergence. We consider it to be part of a revolutionary phase in Bolivia, one whose outcome was never guaranteed but which has brought into being radical historical possibilities, as popular sectors have determined, through the direct assertion of their own power, the parameters for national political and economic development.

In the Plaza San Francisco in La Paz in October, *wiphalas*, the rainbow-colored banner of indigenous self-determination, flapped side by side with tricolored Bolivian flags as Aymara protesters repudiated neoliberal government in the name of the nation. The mingling of these symbols reflected the degree of overlap between Indian and Bolivian identities and between Indian and national-popular struggles today. Some observers scornfully— or fearfully—perceived the recent rebellion as retrograde because of the resurgence of nationalist agendas, or atavistic because of the primacy of indigenous forces in the mobilizations. If the sources of the insurrection were indeed important, so was the originality of this conjuncture. The nascent national-popular bloc no longer revolved around proletarian trade unionism, as it did in earlier twentieth-century movements, but rather acquired an indigenous centrality with a strong rural peasant thrust. The effects of neoliberalism, particularly accelerated urban migration, might have been expected to break down long-standing ethnic solidarities by reinforcing the divide between town and country. Yet instead solidarities were reconstituted, as urban and peri-urban territory was occupied by settlers from the countryside, many of whom retained dual residence in city and country.

The irradiating effects of Indian political struggle were evident in the origins of the urban resistance in September and October, the insurrectionary modes of popular political mobilization, and the cultural memory and identity that galvanized popular insurgents not only in the countryside but in the cities.[7] In September and October 2003, Indian peasant community hunger strikes, road blockades, and confrontations with military forces in the countryside were crucial to the building momentum of the popular movement. During the national mobilization to defend Bolivia's natural resources, government repression led to the death of seven Aymara in Warisata—the historic site of an emancipatory Indian educational center—on 20 September. The murdered were mourned as "martyrs in defense of gas" and peasant community identification with national-popular demands for sovereignty over natural resources opened the way for cross-class, multi-ethnic alliances.

The focus of resistance spread from the countryside to El Alto and semi-urban areas surrounding the capital. These neighborhoods drew upon traditional forms of communal organization and struggle, most notably the tactic of urban siege. The memory of Tupaj Katari, the Aymara peasant commander who led Aymara communities against the Spaniards barricaded within the city of La Paz in 1781, became a potent symbolic force for protesters. The strength of Aymara insurgency, first rural and then urban, empowered other groups with sectoral demands (such as the miners' pension reform or students' call for university autonomy), in addition to the universal demand for control of Bolivian gas. The fifty-four civilians who fell to state violence in El Alto were likewise commemorated as patriotic martyrs, and around the country growing numbers of protestors took up the demands of Aymara insurgents: the resignation of Sánchez de Lozada and his ministers; a trial for those responsible for the killing; a national referendum on how to develop the country's natural gas reserves; the formulation of a new Hydrocarbons Law; and the convening of a National Constituent Assembly.[8]

The presence of the *wiphala* during the uprising signaled the emergence of indigenous political struggle since the 1970s, and the expanding sense of identification with Aymara culture in the Bolivian highlands. According to the 2001 census, 62 percent of the population considered itself indigenous, and the mobilizations since 2000 have only accentuated ethnic identity and political assertiveness. Nationwide, the census found that 25 percent identified as Aymara, 31 percent as Quechua, and 6 percent as one of thirty-one other indigenous groups (Uru-Chipaya, Tupi-Guaraní, etc.). The departments with the highest percentage of indigenous people were Potosí (84 percent), La Paz (78 percent), Cochabamba (74 percent), Oruro (74 percent), Chuquisaca (66 percent), Santa Cruz (38 percent), Beni (33 percent), Tarija (20 percent), Pando (16 percent). The population speaking the Aymara language has been historically concentrated in the Andean highlands, though Aymara migration to the lowlands has increased in the late twentieth century. Speakers of Quechua have predominated in valley regions and highland mining centers, as well as the Chapare lowlands northeast of Cochabamba.

Ethnic self-identification is by no means confined to the countryside. In the city of El Alto, the census found that 74 percent identified as Aymara and 6 percent identified as Quechua, while in urban La Paz the figures were 50 percent and 10 percent, respectively. Nor does it necessarily correspond to mastery of a mother tongue. Though one-fourth of Bolivians identified as Aymara in 2001, for example, 14 percent spoke the language. Though nearly one-third of Bolivians considered themselves Quechua, about one-fifth (21 percent) spoke Quechua. According to World Bank figures, distance between ethnic identification and first language held true in both Guatemala and Peru, where 41 percent identified as indigenous in 2000 and 2001 respectively.[9] By these figures, Bolivia at 62 percent has the highest per capita indigenous population in the Americas.

The underlying national implications of Indian struggle today stem from a structural critique of power relations in the country. Since the national revolution of 1952 was unable to resolve deeper aspects of internal colonialism in Bolivia, indigenous movements hold out the hope that this central contradiction of the republican social formation—the cultural, political, and economic domination of the indigenous majority by a minority mestizo and creole elite—would be addressed finally as the future outlines of the nation are traced.[10] Therein lay the significance of the insurgent demand for a constitutional assembly: through it, and for the first time in republican history, rural and urban indigenous people would be able to reverse patterns of internal colonialism by obtaining democratized, egalitarian forms of political representation at the regional and national levels, and by expanding the domain of communal autonomy and indigenous sovereignty.

Alongside the *wiphala*, what did the Bolivian flag signify during the popular marches and protests? The government's alienation of major natural gas reserves to the transnational corporations Sempra Energy and Pacific LNG, and the recently divulged scheme to export reserves through Chile and potentially to California, had set the stage for the "Gas War" in September and early October 2003. Mobilized popular forces across the country saw this as a repetition of the Bolivian oligarchy's historical betrayal of the nation.

Over centuries, local elites had abetted non-renewable natural resource extraction for colonial and neocolonial accumulation, and in the late nineteenth century they had effectively forfeited Bolivia's nitrate-rich coastal territory to Chile, which has been perceived as an enemy ever since. Protesters were thus objecting to the creole elite's complicity in the appropriation of natural gas—by foreign firms and for foreign markets—as an abrogation of Bolivian sovereignty, which stood to benefit only a small cohort of comprador cronies. Even more galling was the state's willingness to employ lethal violence against an unarmed, mostly Aymara civilian population defending national interests.

Despite mounting challenges to its authority and the rising toll of civilian dead and wounded, the government, with firm backing from the US Embassy, remained determined to hold on to power. This resolution finally dissolved when news arrived on 16 October that the army (most of whose conscripts and lower-level officers are of Quechua-Aymara origin) had decided to let forty-nine truckloads of miners and Quechua-Aymara community peasants from the southern departments of Oruro and Potosí through the checkpoint at Patacamaya (a commercial hub south of La Paz on the road to Oruro). Though even more massive reinforcements for insurgents in El Alto and La Paz were on the way from the provinces, by the time the last of the caravan reached the Plaza San Francisco on 18 October, there was nothing left to do but celebrate, with explosions of dynamite, fight songs, and chants ("Goni, you bastard, the people defeated you!"). Gonzalo Sánchez de Lozada, aka El Gringo because of his US upbringing and American accent, had left La Paz for Miami, fearful of arrest for the killing of nearly seventy people in September and October or of an ugly fate at the hands of popular justice.

After the victory rally in the Plaza San Francisco on 18 October, out-of-towners boarded their trucks to head home. As they reached the upper edge of the city, in La Ceja of El Alto, they had to maneuver slowly around the train cars that had been overturned (by hand) to block the highway from El Alto down to La Paz. Members of El Alto's neighborhood associations (FEJUVE) and the regional workers' central (COR) packed the Avenida 6 de Marzo thoroughfare and the bridges over it, cheering, chanting, and passing foodstuffs, water, coca, and cigarettes to those with a long, cold journey ahead of them. Departing miners and peasants yelled, "When you need help overthrowing another president, just call us!" Given the lack of lasting political articulation between indigenous communities and urban and working-class forces in the past, this moment of convergence and solidarity, symbolized by the crowds in the Plaza San Francisco and Avenida 6 de Marzo in El Alto, was extraordinary though not unprecedented. The capacity to build and sustain political ties across historically deep rural-urban and ethnic-class divides has long been the biggest challenge facing popular forces.

"To Rule by Obeying"

On 21 January 2006, the day before the official inauguration ceremony, Evo Morales Ayma was met by tens of thousands of indigenous community members who gathered at Tiwanaku, an ancient capital of Andean civilization situated just south of Lake Titicaca. Addressing a high-spirited crowd clothed in brightly-colored textiles, and dressed himself in a replica of a thousand-year-old Andean tunic, Morales promised to bring an end to the "colonial and neoliberal model." He appealed for support and guidance: "Control me. If I can't advance, push me, brothers and sisters. Correct me constantly, because I may err." Morales was acknowledging a long-standing Aymara political tradition of control of leaders from the community base, and implicitly recognizing indigenous forces as the true source of his power. Morales also spoke of a "triumph of the democratic and cultural revolution," after a history of exploitation and resistance: "We are in a time of change . . . The time has come to change the evil history of the looting of our natural resources; of discrimination, humiliation, hatred, and contempt."[11] The idea of a "time of change" is one with deep resonance in Andean political culture and has been heard in insurgent moments since the late eighteenth century. In centuries past, community rebels as they rose up echoed the refrain: "The present is a new time," while Indian movements today speak of the present as a *pachakuti*, an overturning of time and space out of which a new phase in history may issue.[12]

The following day, on 22 January, an unprecedented number of Latin American heads of state, visiting dignitaries, and foreign journalists assembled in the congressional building on the Plaza Murillo, the main square of La Paz since colonial times and the central site of state political power since 1899. The occasion was indeed remarkable—in the history of the Americas, it is virtually unheard of for a man of rural Indian origin to become head of state.[13] After being sworn in, Morales called for a moment of silence to honor the martyrs in the pantheon of liberation: Tupaj Katari and Tupaj Amaru, Aymara and Quechua leaders of the anti-colonial revolution of 1781; Zárate Villca, Aymara commander in the Federal War of

1899; Socialist Party leader Marcelo Quiroga Santa Cruz and Jesuit Luis Espinal, both victims of military dictatorship in the early 1980s; and the legendary Che Guevara. In his inauguration speech, Morales emphasized his indigenous identity and its relationship to an insurgent past, as well as his link to the current of Latin American liberation symbolized by Guevara: "I say to you, my Indian brothers and sisters from America concentrated here in Bolivia, the 500-year campaign of resistance has not been in vain. This democratic, cultural fight is part of the fight of our ancestors; it is the continuity of the fight of Tupac Katari, of Che Guevara."[14] A palpable sense of history being made and destiny fulfilled pervaded the dual indigenous and Bolivian ceremonies of inauguration in Tiwanaku and the Plaza Murillo. His own political discourse symbolically located Morales at the point of convergence of two historical traditions of struggle—one indigenous and the other national-popular.

No Bolivian president had ever spoken like this, and the effect was electrifying, especially once it spilled over to the nearby Plaza San Francisco, where perhaps 150,000 Aymara peasants, *alteños* (residents of El Alto), miners, and *paceños* (La Paz residents) from hillside neighborhoods gathered for a rally with "*el compañero presidente*" after the formal ceremony concluded. Vice-President Alvaro García Linera repeated Morales's theme from the previous day: when a long period of oppression was drawing to a close and an era of liberation was beginning to unfold, the newly-elected government would rely on the popular movements for support, guidance, and pressure. In the Plaza San Francisco, tears streamed down the faces of men and women overwhelmed with emotion and the magnitude of their victory.

From 2003 to 2006, a leaderless popular insurrection with a markedly indigenous profile was followed by something else—a legitimate new government with unprecedented indigenous leadership and a national-popular mandate. This new state project was launched with the aspiration and the potential to supersede regnant neoliberal agendas and internal colonial structures. Yet it also carried major risks. One was outright failure, given the daunting obstacles in its path. The other was abandonment of the popular mandate, in the interests of the government's political self-perpetuation.

Evo Morales and Alvaro García Linera were not the only ones to see the electoral victory of the MAS as a historic turning point and revolutionary development. Many national and foreign political commentarists looked upon it in the same way.[15] In our own historical view, the election of Evo Morales did not bring about a revolution. It was a revolution that brought about the government of Evo Morales.

2

Revolution in Historical Context

What's in a Name?

At the end of Shakespeare's drama, Hamlet watches the grave-diggers overturn the soil and heave up from the ground the skulls of unknown men. "Why, that could have been a courtier," he muses, "and this one a politician ... Here's fine revolution, an [if only] we had the trick to see't." In this chapter, we reflect on this problem of seeing revolution even as it has been unfolding in Bolivia. That many observers have not had "the trick to see it" may be due to the messiness of the political process, the difficulty in establishing an external standpoint of evaluation, the narrowness of conventional definitions, or the politically-charged connotations and expectations attached to the term "revolution." We survey here some of the meanings and debates stirred by the current process, and offer our own interpretation of why the overturning and upheaval in Bolivia today should indeed be seen as "fine revolution."

Modern Bolivian history has been marked by powerful insurrections and revolutionary moments, and Adolfo Gilly, historian and long-time witness of revolution in Latin America, called the October insurrection "the first revolution of the twenty-first century."[1] In our view, a phase of insurgency that opened up in 2000 took on a revolutionary dimension in 2003, though the limits of the process were apparent and the range of possible outcomes was broad. This was closer to a national than a socialist revolution, and it was never a foregone conclusion that Indian and popular forces would seize state power directly. Given prevailing skepticism about the possibility for social transformation in the contemporary world, the following synthesis clarifies what we see as revolutionary features of the Bolivian process that came to a head in 2003 and continues to unfold today.

State crisis: After years in which the political legitimacy of state institutions steadily eroded due to neoliberal mismanagement and mounting repression, massive popular mobilizations—uniting groups across class and racial-ethnic lines—ultimately confronted state power head-on, calling for structural transformations of the economy and national political life. First in the department of La Paz, then in other regions, the mobilizations brought about the neutralization of state security forces and the temporary collapse of the established political system—mainstream political parties and executive and legislative branches of government were stripped of legitimacy and effective political power.

Restructuring of political power: Popular pressures not only removed the head of state over United States objections, but also led to conditional approval of a successor whose mandate was to recast modes of accumulation and state-society relations. The result was a profoundly altered balance of forces: without seizing power directly, popular movements, with Aymara women and young people playing leading roles, suddenly exercised substantial, ongoing control from below of state authorities and the state program for national reorganization. The direction of future restructuring was henceforth subject to broadly based national debate.

Transformation of subjectivity: The insurrection also recast political consciousness, as popular groups began to re-conceive both their own roles as historical agents as well as the nation's future. Political power no longer appeared to be alien—the exclusive preserve of professional politicians, corrupt party vehicles, and imperial overlords. Among emerging conceptions of the nation were radical Aymara visions of separatist autonomy, dual power in which Indian authorities would share control over the state, or hegemony in a country of majority indigenous population. The solidification of ethnic and national-popular identities along with the imagination of a more democratic future were fired by the political memory of past struggles: rural communities and urban Aymara in El Alto took inspiration from the anti-colonial Andean insurrection of 1780–1, while middle-class protesters briefly reenacted the hunger strike that brought down the García Meza dictatorship in 1981.

Counter-revolution: As radical aspirations for change arose, especially among rural and urban Aymara, elites and conservative middle-class fractions in the capital tended to retreat, expressing their vulnerability and anxiety by forming neighborhood militias designed to protect lives and property, both of which were imagined to be under threat. In Bolivia's east and southeast, racist pronouncements and proposals for regional autonomy, directly opposed to those emerging in the western highlands, began to circulate. After 17 October, displaced political forces from the neoliberal right promptly began plotting to undermine the new government as well as popular leaders, and used their ongoing institutional influence to step up efforts to criminalize social movements under the guise of the "war on drugs and terror." Counter-revolutionary memory, recalling earlier experiences of indigenous siege, was likewise activated in conservative circles during and after October.

This therefore constitutes the third major revolutionary moment in "Bolivian" history. The first in the southern Andean territory that is today Bolivia was indigenous. Starting in August of 1780, a regional insurgency in Potosí under the leadership of an Indian commoner named Tomás Katari set off a chain of regional movements. These insurgencies have come to be known for the involvement of the descendant of Inka royalty, José Gabriel Tupaj Amaru, who symbolically headed the insurrection in the southern Peruvian region of Cuzco. The highlands of Oruro and La Paz ignited in early 1781, and Aymara and Quechua troops cleared the countryside of Spanish colonial control. The Aymara peasant commander in La Paz, Tupaj Katari, strangled Spanish forces holding out in the city of La Paz, in a siege lasting five months in all. Yet lacking urban allies, Indian troops never succeeded in taking the city. In late 1781, royalist counter-insurgency forces sent from the viceregal capital of Buenos Aires arrived to defeat the Quechua-Aymara army. Katari was drawn and quartered, and Spanish authorities held on to colonial rule until they were definitively overthrown in 1825. Among elites within the city as well as Aymara protesters, the sieges of La Paz in September 2000, October 2003, and June 2005 recalled the great anti-colonial insurrection of over two centuries ago.

The second great revolution in Bolivia was also the first national-popular revolution in postwar Latin America. In April 1952, the middle-class National Revolutionary Movement (MNR) backed by the armed force of Trotskyist (POR) workers from the Catavi tin mines, led a dramatic three-day urban insurrection. The revolution brought an end to the oligarchic rule that had prevailed since the early nineteenth century, and the temporary destruction of the landlord class, the nationalization of the mines, and the universal extension of the franchise. The agrarian reform secured for the MNR the political loyalty of the peasantry, while miners were incorporated into a nationally coordinated trade union apparatus closely linked to center-left sectors of the MNR. State firms managed the extraction and export of strategic natural resources, especially minerals and petroleum. The mixed model of state capitalism lasted, with alternation between MNR dominance in the political sphere and de facto authoritarian military regimes, until the tin market collapse and neoliberal restructuring of 1985.

Bolivia's third revolutionary moment came at a time of Andean regional instability and the crumbling of the Washington Consensus in the first years of the twenty-first century. Yet the Bolivian experience cannot be taken simply as the predictable effect of broad international or structural causes. "Neoliberalism" is not an automatic force that inevitably transforms local societies and thereby gives rise to its own "grave-diggers."[2]

One of our arguments is that the current resistance is deeply rooted in non-liberal forms of collective organization—*ayllus* and peasant communities, neighborhood associations, market vendors' associations, regional trade union centrals, the miners' union, coca growers' trade union federations—that have long been central to the daily lives of the majority of Bolivians. These forms of organization, under constant and apparently successful attack since neoliberal structural adjustment began in 1985, yield modes of struggle familiar from subaltern political history and, surprisingly, still present today. A matrix of indigenous community politics formed in the anti-colonial struggles of the late eighteenth century has shaped contemporary patterns of communal insurgency and base-level control over political representatives.[3] Even with the decline of the once powerful Bolivian Workers' Central (COB) and the "relocation" of the vanguard mine workers, traditions of trade union politics engrained over the course of the twentieth century have been transmitted to new popular organizations and younger generations. Hence when Bolivians began the latest cycle of resistance and insurgency in 2000, their radical traditions of organizing provided unexpected reserves of strength. Revolutionary forces and aspirations, only recently thought to have been buried, resurfaced suddenly, with remarkable energy and creativity, albeit in new forms and under new circumstances.

The power, depth, and revolutionary content of the October insurrection resulted from a rare convergence between Indian and national-popular horizons. The memory of 1952–3 seemed obsolete after the revolution's own frustrations as well as the imposition of neoliberalism since 1985. Unexpectedly however, a new national revolutionary horizon, brought into being with insurgent Aymara initiative, has opened up in the twenty-first century. This reflects recent struggles (2000–6), the vivid memory of more distant ones (1781), and may further reawaken some of the national-popular demands—especially regarding national sovereignty over natural resources—associated with 1952.[4] The process proved surprising to virtually all political analysts, not to mention the political class that had managed the Bolivian state through party coalitions after neoliberal restructuring began. Even those who now emphasize the revolutionary character of the current conjuncture realize that the future contours of the republic remain blurry. Regardless of subsequent developments, however, this radical shift needs to be understood in terms of the cycles of Bolivia's revolutionary past, the memory and forgetting of previous revolutionary moments, and the tension-filled connections between indigenous and national-popular political expressions.

Bolshevik Ghosts

The startlingly swift overthrow of Sánchez de Lozada—by "grave-diggers" on the altiplano, in the city of El Alto, and subsequently throughout the provinces—inspired enormous enthusiasm and expectation of change. While some participants and witnesses began to describe the "Days of October" as revolutionary, other media pundits and political analysts shied away from such fraught language. They preferred to guard a sober tone, either masking anxiety about the consequences or seeking to avoid populist bombast and associations with utopian romance.

From the beginning, many observers pointed to the missing ingredient: if the old regime had been toppled, there had been no seizure of the state by insurgent forces. Naturally, this was the position from more traditional and revolutionary left perspectives. Vice-President Carlos Mesa had replaced Sánchez de Lozada, through a constitutional process of succession, and Mesa represented the continuation of neoliberalism, even if he pledged not to spill more civilian blood. According to this outlook, there had been no vanguard leadership to direct the insurrection and to channel its energies towards a new revolutionary state. Both Trotskyists and radical Indianists, in many other respects at odds with each other, converged in accusing Evo Morales and the MAS of betrayal of the revolution. Morales was nowhere to be seen when the social mobilizations began to gain momentum, and he had lagged behind the popular movement, including the base of his own party, in voicing demands to restructure the hydro-carbon industry.

Of course for traditional sectors of the revolutionary left, the absence of proletarian hegemony in the popular movement was confounding as well. But for those who did not assume that MAS or a proletarian vanguard organization was ripe for such a role, the question remained as to why Boli-vian popular movements had been able to mount such potent resistance vis-à-vis the right or governing regimes historically, yet been unable to seize the levers of the state and exercise authority directly. By these standards, the Days of October were impressive and inspiring in many ways, but disappointing or incomplete in others. They certainly were no revolution.

By Any Other Name

There were also alternative conceptions of October. When Adolfo Gilly called for an unblinkered view of the insurrection as "the first revolution of the twenty-first century," he cited the definition of revolution that Lenin penned in July 1917:

> The bourgeois revolution in Russia from 1905 to 1907, although it never achieved the same "brilliant" successes like the ones obtained in certain moments of the Turkish and Portuguese revolutions, was undoubtedly a truly popular revolution, as the mass of the people, the majority of them, the lowest social strata, crushed by oppression and exploitation, rose up of their own initiative and marked the whole course of the revolution with the stamp of *their* demands, *their* efforts to build, in their own way, the new society, in place of the old society which needs to be destroyed.[5]

Gilly's outlook captured the sentiment of many who had lived through the vertiginous process of insurgency and counter-insurgency, although some Bolivians were taken aback at the claim when his analysis filtered into public political discourse.[6]

The term conjures up a range of connotations. In the interests of clarity, and along the same sight-line as Gilly, we view the latest cycle as part of a "*social revolution*," that had the October insurrection as its most defining moment. In this sense, our notion of the revolutionary nature of October also approximates Trotsky's classic formulation:

> The most indubitable feature of a revolution is the direct interference of the masses in historic events. In ordinary times the state, be it monarchical or democratic, elevates itself above the nation, and history is made by specialists in that line of business—kings, ministers, bureaucrats, parliamentarians, journalists. But at those crucial moments when the old order becomes no longer endurable to the masses, they break over the barriers excluding them from the political arena, sweep aside their traditional representatives, and create by their own interference the initial groundwork for a new regime.[7]

At the same time, we view this third revolution broadly as a *conjuncture* and *process* rather than a single event, such as the takeover of the state. It is a process whose outcome was not given in advance. After October 2003, it was by no means foreseeable that MAS would come to power, and no less plausible that the right would regain control over the state through counter-insurgent reaction or through the exhaustion of popular forces.

Our own understanding of the revolutionary process, then, emphasizes the *insurrectionary* aspect of October—"the direct interference of the masses in historic events"—as reconfiguring the national political arena. The features of popular mobilization during the insurgencies beginning in 2000 closely resembled modes, mechanisms, and dynamics of indigenous insurgency in earlier episodes of southern Andean history. Elsewhere, we have sought to identify a distinctive "insurrectionary political culture" that can be traced back to the eighteenth century and followed up until the twentieth. This was only one dimension of a broader range and repertoire of indigenous political engagements (which included strategies of alliances, pacts, and legal action), and it was not a continuous phenomenon, but one which recurred historically, given the political limitations for indigenous people in an internal colonial formation. It was based on enduring, everyday dynamics of communal organization. This indigenous insurrectionary political culture was also one that helped shape popular and urban insurrections historically.[8]

Bolivian and other Latin American authors have done much to illuminate contemporary political struggles in Bolivia in ways that challenge certain traditional left assumptions about revolution. These are accounts that center less on vanguard political leaderships and the battle for state power, which we might loosely term "Bolshevik" here (despite the lucid definitions of the Bolshevik thinkers cited above). Rather, some of these accounts would be closer to "anarchist" positions skeptical of concentrated political authority in the state and stressing the dynamism of communal democracy and local-regional collective action. Some privilege the role of grassroots social movements in the renewal of the left after its long association with vanguard party and centralized trade union structures. Related Indianist positions assert a key emancipatory role for indigenous cultural and political movements. On this last point, the Zapatista project in Chiapas, Mexico, that inspired new political outlooks among activists and social movements internationally in the 1990s, overlaps with indigenous agendas in Bolivia.[9]

A central feature of such analyses has been attention to the self-organization, local self-government, and autonomous spaces forged by mobilized popular forces in the countryside and cities since 2000. During the siege of La Paz, for example, neighborhood associations—drawing on communal and trade union traditions of insurgency—acquired a key role in El Alto. They became the forum for collective decision-making, the designation of representatives, and the coordination of direct actions. Like rural communities at the same time, the urban associations operated on a rotating basis to provide contingents of protesters, foodstuffs, and materiel for marches, barricades, and self-defense. In the phases of intensive mobilization, direct action was carried out in the absence of a general command structure. Felipe Quispe—the radical Aymara leader known as "El Mallku" ("The Condor") who headed the Bolivian Peasant Trade Union Confederation (CSUTCB)—certainly helped prepare the ground and supplied a radical discourse for rural insurgents. Yet he had no capacity to orient action once the mobilization was under way. In the city, neighborhood organizations turned into what Aymara sociologist Pablo Mamani calls "territorial micro-governments." The population responded to changing conditions through its own base-level initiatives. It did not answer to vertical bureaucratic hierarchy, such as the executive authority of the FEJUVE or the COR, or to caudillo or party leadership, such as that of Evo Morales or MAS, as government officials insinuated.

The mounting process of insurgency also brought about a takeover of resources, territory, and even political and military control from the state. Urban and regional protests asserted people's rights to shape natural resource policy and management. This was evident in the Water War in Cochabamba, the expulsion of the French water company Suez Lyonnais in El Alto, or the takeover of foreign-run gas fields in the lowlands. The marches, road blockades, land seizures, and urban sieges shut down ground circulation in different parts of the country, and made large swathes of highland territory inaccessible even for military forces. Insurgents also expelled subprefectural, mayoral, police, and judicial (*registro civil*) author-ities, freed prisoners from local jails, and burned down state offices in some highland towns. In the Yungas valleys northeast of La Paz, peasant trade unions repelled the intervention of the Joint Task Force (a militarized drug police), and in Kurawara and Achacachi, communities challenged and isolated the military battalions stationed in their territory. Just as coca-growers in the Chapare had created self-defense committees in the 1990s, community police forces, representing the CSUTCB and Indian authority, formed in the provincial capitals of the highlands. The CSUTCB came to declare its own state of siege, and Aymara forces set up the General Headquarters of Qalachaka, a regional military command post representing hundreds of communities. These experiences of autonomous grassroots direct action were taken by some as the embryonic equivalent of revolutionary "soviets" and as effective instances of "dual power" that could be built upon to create an alternative to the existing state form.[10]

Thus, in the aftermath of the Days of October, a spectrum of opinion emerged as to the revolutionary dimension of what had occurred, and opinions were divided over the achievements and limits of the insurrection. For some, the crucial limitation was the popular movement's inability to seize the state, due to the absence of truly revolutionary leadership. For the sake of debate, we have framed such a position here as "Bolshevik," although it applied equally to some indigenous militants. For others, closer to an "anarchist" position, this non-state orientation and the lack of a concerted political hierarchy were less the weaknesses than the strengths of a powerful insurgent popular movement.

With the election of Evo Morales, the tables on this debate were turned. Contrary to "Bolshevik" expectations, social movements gained an unprecedented degree of political representation in state government and executive office. More than ever before, popular forces stood to exercise control over levers of the state. At the same time, the new situation posed challenges to positions we have referred to as "anarchist," since the focus of political energy largely shifted from grassroots to national political levels. For both traditional and new radical perspectives, what was unexpected was that the latest advance of popular forces should come through electoral rather than insurrectionary channels. Meanwhile, even mainstream media were caught up in Evo-mania, as commentators acknowledged the revolutionary quality of the transformation. One Bolivian analyst, only half ironically, declared, "From now on, Bolivian history will be divided in two parts: before Evo Morales and after him."[11]

Morales and his Vice-President Alvaro García Linera issued high-powered rhetorical statements after the election, which resonated loudly in the media, to the effect that a true "revolution" had in fact come about and a historic new era was dawning. This was a "revolution in democracy," a "revolution by the ballot box not the rifle." Said the new president: "We're taking over now for the next 500 years. We're going to put an end to injustice, to inequality." After the convocation of the constitutional assembly in March 2006, Morales asserted, "The *jach'a uru* [millennial great day] is near!"

In assessing such discourse and claims, it is important to recognize the government's stated aims, and not simply judge it by external criteria. The historic transformation claimed by MAS—despite, or perhaps in keeping, with its "movement to socialism" moniker—was not a "socialist" revolution. It was a cultural and political revolution to "decolonize" the state, by bringing into being national political representation and leadership for the indigenous majority. It was a project for autonomy or self-rule, not at the communal or municipal level alone, but at the highest levels of government. Hence MAS's congressional bloc after the December 2006 elections consisted of 72 representatives of whom 43 were indigenous; 12 senators of whom 3 were indigenous (and one female). Its first cabinet included 4 indigenous people (two of whom were women). Finally, the head of state was Aymara, of peasant extraction, while his vice-president came from the white urban middle class. This indigenous project of government—a significant break even from much *cocalero*, peasant, and trade union discourse in the past— was also evoked by the government's pledge to "rule by obeying" (*mandar obedeciendo*). The use of this slogan appeared to be a nod to the Zapatista rebellion in Chiapas, which coined it to express an alternative conception of political leadership. Yet it is consonant with practices of communal indigenous political culture in Bolivia that can be traced back to the anti-colonial movements of the eighteenth century.[12]

As detailed in chapter eleven, the historical process moved beyond one of a classic situation of dual power, whether of a "soviet" or indigenous-communal sort, beyond an anarchist, social movement, or other grassroots model grounded in a clear opposition to state power. Morales himself asserted that his was a "government of the social movements," and did not resign his position as head of the *cocalero* trade union federations of the Chapare, as he was expected to do in order to become the "president of all Bolivians." Instead he accepted re-election, presumably as a signal that he would not cut himself off from the social movements, that he continued as their legitimate representative. The new situation therefore confounded more "anarchist" scenarios, and forced the state-social movement relationship back onto the agenda, though in unexpected fashion.

Ancestral Spirits

"Bolshevik" and "anarchist" categories can serve for purposes of debate, but in the Andean context, notions of "revolution" are also expressed in a native tongue. The Quechua-Aymara term *pachakuti* can be interpreted as a profound turning or transformation of the world (space and time). The term has become a keyword in the Andes since the 1970s, as ethno-historians and indigenous intellectuals—with both overlap and friction between the two—explored the term's meaning in Andean culture histor-ically and employed it for its present-day political resonance.[13] For those who identify with indigenous movements, the notion invokes a time-cycle corresponding to the five hundred years elapsed since the Spanish conquest—1992 was a moment of particular efflorescence for this historical imaginary. If the conquest was a cataclysmic rupture that brought about European ascendancy and indigenous subordination, today it means a turning of the world right side up. It carries distinctly cosmic connotations, heralding a new time for humans and nature alike, but there is no clear distinction made between realms of the sacred and the mundane. It does not suggest that cosmic change occurs on a plane distinct from that of political change; rather, the two are indissolubly linked. The insurgencies since 2000 and the unprecedented experience of an Indian head of state have intensified this sensation of entering a new historical era.

The power of historical and mythical memory in Bolivia might seem to confirm Marx's own dictum about past revolutions. Marx described how, time and again, revolutionaries have dressed themselves up in worn out attire in order to make themselves presentable: "Just when they seem engaged in revolutionizing themselves and things, in creating something entirely new, precisely in such epochs of revolutionary crisis they anxiously conjure up the spirits of the past to their service and borrow from them names, battle slogans and costumes in order to present the new scene of world history in this time-honored disguise and this borrowed language."

For Marx, writing about France in his own time, this historical rehearsal was tragic in 1789 and farcical in 1848, but in both cases the failure of imagination reflected a failure of nerve: "Earlier revolutions required world-historical recollections in order to drug themselves concerning their own content." Marx's vision of the coming revolution stressed a total break with the past—all that "old crap," as he once called it—and a shedding of the weight of history, for "the tradition of all the dead generations weighs like a nightmare on the brain of the living." Marx thus enjoined the new revolutionary generation to "let the dead bury their dead." A forgetting was required in order to achieve a confident new self-expression: "The beginner who has learnt a new language always translates it back into his mother tongue, but he has assimilated the spirit of the new language and produces freely in it only when he moves in it without remembering the old and forgets in it his ancestral tongue."[14]

In light of Bolivian experiences of revolution in the twenty-first century, however, we view the matter differently. The Bolivian revolutionary process has drawn much of its power by re-creating the past symbolically so as to transform the present—making history not only in the sense of influencing the course of events, but also of producing the meaning of events. One of the lessons we can take from the Bolivian and Zapatista examples is that revolutionary processes today feature reconnection with a long-negated, underground history that has scarcely begun to be written.

The point, then, is not to bury the dead, but to rouse the spirits of the ancestors so that they may return to the world to animate present-day struggles. Tupaj Katari himself traveled to the pre-conquest Aymara tombs still standing on the altiplano and called out: "Now is the time to return to the world to help me!" The ancestral language of *pachakuti* likewise implies a re-turning to a new beginning. It is in this sense, and not as sheer regression, that the past can be seen as a future. History is thus much more than the nightmare of Tupaj Katari's dismemberment, or the vile murder of nineteenth-century Aymara leader Zárate Villca. Re-membering and re-animating Andean history incites dream visions of a different, better future; visions that inspire collective action.

Revolutionary Horizons

To restate our position: we do not posit unchanging revolutionary visions or essences of ancient origin unique to Indian movements in the southern Andes. Our point, precisely, is that like revolution itself, the *meaning* of revolution changes over time as part of a dynamic, open-ended process that unfolds under particular conditions of time and place. But within change, we can see recurrent figures and patterns in the historical tapestry, which is constantly being enlarged and woven anew.

One lesson we might take from our look at "Bolshevik" and "anarchist" positions is that historical dynamics will always exceed and confound fixed, static conceptions of the world. Revolutionary processes themselves point up the inadequacy of conventional concepts and understandings of "revolution." They expose our limited imagination when we stick too fast to our own judgments about the successes or failures of revolutions themselves. Marx himself warned against the pitfalls of trans-historical models and theories: "Success will never come with the master-key of a general historico-philosophical theory, whose supreme virtue consists in being supra-historical."[15] Such critical awareness is essential, yet it need not keep us from pursuing theoretically-informed historical explanation. In what follows, then, we ground our narrative in local processes and track political subjects over more than two centuries to discern more clearly the shape of the present.

In this book, we approach revolutionary "horizons" not only as those perspectives of men and women in the past who looked out upon the possibilities for future social transformation. For there is also another sense of the word. At an archeological site, the phased strata of the earth and the remains of human settlement that are exposed by careful digging are also called "horizons." We offer this then as an excavation of Andean revolution, whose successive layers of historical sedimentation comprise the subsoil, loam, landscape, and vistas for current political struggle in Bolivia.

PART II

Internal Colonialism and Insurgency, 1781–1984

Commemoration of the Dead, El Alto, October 2004. © Noah Friedman-Rudovsky

3

Indian Rule and Creole Rule in the Age of Revolution, 1781–1825

The project of Indian political sovereignty at its most expansive—associated with Aymara radicalism in our own time—was first envisioned as part of anti-colonial struggles in the eighteenth century. These culminated in 1780–1 in the southern Andes' first revolutionary moment—the most powerful anti-colonial movement in Latin America prior to independence. One smoldering region after another ignited: Northern Potosí under Tomás Katari, Cuzco under Tupaj Amaro, Oruro, and finally La Paz under Tupaj Katari. This insurrection in the Andes took place shortly after anti-colonial warfare wracked North America, and shortly before social revolution would overwhelm France and its precious jewel in the Caribbean, Haiti. Over the course of one full year, the political future of the Andean highlands hung in the balance. Manuel de Godoy, the prime minister of Carlos IV (1788–1808), subsequently wrote: "No one ignores how close we were to losing, around the years 1781 and 1782, the entire Viceroyalty of Peru and part of the Viceroyalty of Río de La Plata when the standard of insurrection was raised by the famous Condorcanqui, better known by the name of Tupac-Amaro, answered and aided in the province of La Paz by the bloody Tupa-Catari."

The insurrectionary territory in 1780–1 was centered in the Aymara and Quechua heartland of what is today southern Peru and Bolivia. Yet the repercussions reached far beyond this, down the Andean cordillera into Argentina, along the coastal stretch of northern Chile, into the Amazonian mission districts of Bolivia, and up through the Peruvian highlands to Ecuador and Colombia (again, borrowing terminology and borders from contemporary national geography). "The waves of the storm," according to Godoy, were even felt as far away as Mexico.

In the core territory, from Cuzco down to beyond Potosí, the countryside and the provincial capitals in the highlands were largely cleared of Spanish state control. By Godoy's estimates, rebel armies marshaled 80,000 Indian combatants, 20,000 of them armed, and a number of creoles and mestizos contributed to the cause.[1] Only in the cities—Cuzco itself, La Paz, Oruro, and Potosí—did colonial elites hold out, staving off Indian siege and eking out a miserable existence while hoping their prayers would be heard in the distant courts of the colonial state.

By late 1781, royalist armies sent from Lima and Buenos Aires eventually managed to put down the concerted projects for a new Andean, Indian, and communal sovereignty. One key to the fortunes of the movement was the projected alliance between indigenous forces and creole and mestizo allies. When this alliance failed to coalesce or broke down, in one region after another, it proved fateful for the revolution as a whole. A few decades later, anti-colonial war would again burst forth and this time lead to independence from the European overlord. Yet the historical outcome would be drastically different. The political leadership and designs were those of creole elites, while more radical aspirations for Indian power and self-rule were buried underfoot.

Undermining Empire

After the initial phase of Spanish conquest beginning in the 1530s and the internecine Spanish wars over the spoils, Peruvian Viceroy Francisco de Toledo consolidated a stable regime in the Andes by the 1570s. The basis of the colonial order was a state-community pact in which diverse native peoples, now lumped together under the rubric of "Indians," provided labor and tribute to the Spanish crown in exchange for protection of their land base and a relative degree of local autonomy. Using a strategy of indirect rule, Spain appointed ethnic authorities called *caciques*, drawn from the hereditary Andean nobility, as intermediaries to govern densely settled local populations.

By the middle of the eighteenth century, however, colonial rule in the southern Andes had begun to unravel. In the former domain of the Inka state, one of the two most important centers of native population in the Americas, a set of new historical conditions—foremost among them imperial restructuring, intensified modes of economic extraction, and increasingly tenacious indigenous resistance—undermined established forms of colonial domination. Anxious to keep up with its northern Atlantic imperial rivals, England and France, the Bourbon monarchy introduced over decades a series of reforms designed to overhaul its imperial administration. Under Carlos III (1759–88), the most significant measures in the Andes included more efficient collection of Indian tribute, increased taxation of trade in the 1770s, and the creation of the new Viceroyalty of La Plata in 1776. The administrative jurisdiction of Charcas—which was known commonly as Upper Peru in the colonial period and which would form the territorial basis for the post-colonial state of Bolivia—was separated from the Viceroyalty of Peru, with its court in Lima, and incorporated into the new Viceroyalty of La Plata with its court in Buenos Aires.

The Bourbon reform project met with mixed success and, ironically, some of its apparent achievements—such as increased fiscal extraction—provoked alienation, political realignments, and social unrest among different groups within New World society. Indians, mestizos, and creoles were all involved in urban agitation or open revolts over commercial taxation and regulation in Cochabamba in 1774, La Paz in 1777 and 1778, and Arequipa, Cuzco, and La Paz again in 1780.[2]

The most onerous institution for Indians in the eighteenth century was the forced distribution of commodities (*reparto de mercancías*), which fused commercial capital with colonial state power to siphon huge surpluses from indigenous peasant community labor. In this system, provincial Spanish governors known as *corregidores* took commodities on credit from merchants, and delivered them to Indians who were obliged to accept and then repay them over time at a higher cost. The *corregidores* set up networks of agents and debt-collectors who exercised increasingly tight control over local communities, and they cajoled or coerced Indian community authorities, the *caciques*, into compliance with the system. This private enterprise was illegal yet tolerated and increasingly common from the 1690s on. After the Crown legalized the practice in the 1750s, in order to take its own cut from the profits through taxation, the exploitation intensified.[3] As established norms of moral economy and political mediation between the state and communities were transformed, local conflicts proliferated in the highlands and highland valleys after the 1730s.

In order to defend themselves, peasants combined recourse to the

Bourbon judicial system with direct action to challenge abusive Spanish officials, to take advantage of new cleavages among colonial elites, and replace their own traitorous authorities when they collaborated with exploitative outsiders.[4] Even in the early 1770s, after notorious attacks against *corregidores* and *caciques* in provincial capitals such as Sicasica, Chulumani, and Caquiaviri, the state's ability to quash or isolate local resistance led it to overestimate its powers and postpone meaningful reforms of ingrained abuses. By this point, though there was no coordinated anti-colonial movement in the southern Andes, the spread of local conflicts undermined the system of indirect rule through *caciques* and contributed to state crisis in the countryside.

With established forms of hereditary authority and centralized *cacique* leadership breaking down, a process of democratization was taking place within indigenous communities in this same period. Political power was devolving towards the base of communities and dispersing among multiple sites. Key decisions were arrived at in assembly, offices were held on an annual rotating basis, and authorities were held in check and expected to adopt an ethos of service. These forms of communal democracy would shape patterns of indigenous mobilization in the eighteenth century, and mark community politics and culture until the present.[5]

Overturning Empire

In this agitated century, amidst the swirling local conflict over abusive authorities and onerous exactions, and as established local and supra-local political legitimacies eroded, anti-colonial critiques and visions of self-rule circulated widely and openly, taking various forms. In conspiracies and revolts up and down the Andean cordillera, insurgents imagined a range of possible political orders. The most striking project was for the restoration of the Inka royal dynasty, truncated—illegitimately in popular perception—by Spanish conquest. Under the Inka, rebels hoped to unite the descendants of the pre-conquest Indian nobility, the great masses of the peasantry, as well as disgruntled mestizos and creoles. In 1739 in Oruro, Juan Vélez de Córdoba headed a small band of creoles and *caciques* who sought to "liberate the homeland (*patria*), purging it of the tyranny of the *guampos*" (a native term for peninsular Spaniards) and to "re-establish the great empire and monarchy of our ancient kings."[6]

Yet in Upper Peru or Charcas, as Bolivian territory was then known, the Inka presence had been relatively thin prior to conquest. Hence many Indian peasants imagined an Andean utopia that did not involve the return of the Inka. Peasant anti-colonial visions included the notion that Indians could enjoy equality with Spaniards as well as communal autonomy under the crown. Another project anticipated coexistence among Indians and Spaniards yet under communal Indian hegemony. This was pursued in a number of cases, such as the town of Caquiaviri to the east of La Paz in 1771, when Indians seized power and forced local townspeople to dress in native clothing, to swear a vow of loyalty, and to fight and serve the community within which they were ritually inducted. If these options failed, another agenda called for the outright expulsion or elimination of the colonial Spanish adversary. In the late 1740s and early 1750s, rebels in Chuani, a highland community east of Lake Titicaca, aimed "to wipe out or dominate the *viracochas*" (a Quechua term used to refer to Spaniards since the time of the conquest), and believed that "through force they will overcome everyone, even those of the province, because it is their turn to rule." Often these movements reflected a collective memory of former freedom, or a sense that a historic time of transformation for Indians had finally arrived.[7]

Decades of local political conflict, state crisis, and deepening disaffection with the colonial order came to a head in 1780 when Indian communities rose up in the greatest anti-colonial revolution yet seen in the Americas.[8] The first in a chain of regional insurgencies emerged in northern Potosí after years of simmering conflict involving the *corregidor* and his *cacique* accomplices. A peasant from the town of Macha, Tomás Katari, took up the defense of local communities and appealed to Bourbon officials in La Plata (today Sucre), site of the district's judicial tribunal, and as far away as Buenos Aires, seat of the new viceroyalty for Charcas. After a remarkable journey to obtain Viceroy Juan José de Vértiz's recognition and legal support, Katari outmaneuvered despotic local and regional officials to enforce "his law and his justice." With the local state collapsing due to its internal contradictions and illegitimacy in the eyes of the Indian populace, Katari filled the political vacuum and acquired effective governing authority as well as popular acclaim throughout the region.

After Aymara communities in Northern Potosí had risen up and captured their *corregidor* Joaquín de Alós in August 1780, it was in the Cuzco region that insurgent forces next challenged the colonial power structure. José Gabriel Condorcanqui, *cacique* in the town of Tinta and nearby towns of Surimana and Tungasuca, captured and hung *Corregidor* Antonio de Arriaga in early November. Condorcanqui claimed descent from the last Inka monarch Tupaj Amaru who had been executed by Viceroy Toledo in 1572, and therefore assumed the name Tupaj Amaru for himself. Amaru initially asserted that he was acting to punish bad government in the name of King Carlos III of Spain. Yet his own royal self-presentation in the countryside and his popular reception as Inka King belied this political stratagem.

Tupaj Amaru advocated a series of reforms designed to overhaul colonial society. All government authorities guilty of corruption and abuse would be deposed. In particular, Indian officials termed *alcaldes mayores* would take over as provincial magistrates governing in lieu of the *corregidores.* Forced consumption and state sales monopolies would be eliminated. Trade restrictions would be repealed, and the widely resented customs-houses and commercial taxes would be abolished. Forced labor in the mines of Potosí and in textile shops, both despised forms of bonded Indian labor, would be brought to an end. Freedom would be granted to slaves who joined Amaru's cause.

Even more radically, Amaru called for a cross-class, interethnic alliance that would unite Indians with mestizos and creoles in order to throw off the "heavy yoke that for so many years they had suffered" and to expel the European overlords. This may be seen as a proto-national project, bringing together under restored Inka sovereignty the different members of colonial society who were born in the Americas. In fact, alongside his immediate coterie of kin and dissident *caciques,* Amaru's military camp included a substantial number of creoles and mestizos serving as administrators, scribes, and arms manufacturers.

Tupaj Amaru emerged as the symbolic leader of insurrection throughout the Andes. Though the actual radius of his political control was limited to the Quechua-speaking regions north of Lake Titicaca, word of his authority spread rapidly. Other regions waited expectantly for the imminent arrival of the conquering Inka redeemer. On the southern altiplano, Amaru's call to alliance seemed to bear fruit in early February 1781. Community insurgents invaded the mining city of Oruro where they were received by creoles and mestizos welcoming them as "brothers, friends, comrades." While Indians and plebeians attacked the peninsular Spaniards in the city, an interim government formed under Jacinto Rodriguez, a creole who now donned an Inka tunic.

Yet those non-Indians who were initially drawn to the movement—whether out of conviction, perceived interest, or sheer fright—soon backed away. Tentative, fragile ties quickly frayed as creoles realized the limits of their own power within the movement, the strength of mobilized peasant community forces, as well as the military vulnerability of the insurgents. As mistrust deepened and the alliance broke down, the political conflict sharpened and polarized increasingly along ethnic lines. In mid-February, creole leaders took up weapons, drove their erstwhile Indian comrades from the city, and made common cause with the peninsular Spaniards. Thereafter radicalized communities would strike back in counter-attacks against the traitorous *q'aras* (an Aymara term for parasitic exploiters that was applied now equally to mestizos, creoles, and peninsular Spaniards).

The movement in La Paz burst open in March 1781 under the vigorous command of Julián Apaza, an unknown Aymara commoner. Apaza assumed a mantle of concentrated political, military, and spiritual authority, and adopted the name Tupaj Katari (meaning Resplendent Serpent) in order to identify himself with the prestigious leaders from Potosí and Cuzco. Katari and his consort Bartolina Sisa set up their court in El Alto, on the shelf overlooking the great basin of La Paz. Aymara communities throughout the region rose up laying waste to Spanish enemies, and besieging royalist forces barricaded in the city of La Paz. Indian troops were encouraged by Katari's promises that "they would be left as the ultimate owners of this place, and of its wealth." They confidently expected the imminent occasion upon which "Indians alone would rule."[9] Katari issued invitations to creole and mestizo "compatriots" to abandon the royalist encampment and join the insurgent cause. Yet he had fewer such "compatriots" in his own camp than did Amaru, and as conflict surged in the aftermath of the rupture in Oruro, there was dwindling hope for such a cross-class, interethnic project.

A minority of *caciques* and members of the Inka nobility rallied to the call of Tupaj Amaru in Cuzco, though most stood firmly in support of the crown. In Upper Peru, virtually all *caciques* sided with the Spanish cause, while radicalism intensified at the base level as political and "racial" polarization grew. Andean peasant communities rose up as unified and formidable forces, drawing on decades of accumulated experience of mobilization. They sought to extend the domains of political autonomy they had fought for in prior local struggles against *caciques* and *corregidores*. As a result of the ongoing process of internal democratization in the eighteenth century, in which *cacique* authority devolved and dispersed throughout the community, base-level forces played a powerful role in determining the political will and decisions in 1781. This effect was most evident in Oruro, where no outstanding leadership emerged to direct mobilized communities. Yet the bottom-up dynamic in power relations was also the case in La Paz. It was no coincidence that Tupaj Katari was from the lowest stratum of indigenous society. His fierce warrior conduct reflected an aspect of Andean peasant political culture and, as he testified himself, was a reaction to the radicalism of the community forces under his command.

After Tupaj Amaru's capture by Spanish troops near Tinta in April 1781, his Quechua colonels from the north swept down into the Lake Titicaca arena and converged with Aymara troops, thereby converting the region into the most important theater in the second phase of the Andean revolutionary war. Tupaj Amaru's proud young nephew, Andrés Mendigure, and Katari's sister, Gregoria Apaza, who became an esteemed leader in her own right, became lovers and together seized Sorata, the capital of Larecaja province. They then arrived to bolster Katari's siege of La Paz. Over a period of 184 days, between March and June and then again between August and October, residents of the city suffered constant attack as well as punishing famine, disease, and despair. The memory of this period would later grip urban creoles and mestizos subject to recurrent Indian sieges in the nineteenth, twentieth, and early twenty-first centuries.

Ultimately, however, Katari and his Quechua allies were unable to vanquish Spanish troops holding out in the city. Indian forces had the strength of numbers on their side, and displayed remarkable unity in mobilization as well as tenacity in combat. However, the failure to win over creole, mestizo, or urban plebeian allies limited an insurgent cause that possessed few military resources of its own. Peasant troops were untrained, scarcely armed, and hindered by costly tactical errors on the part of their commanders. Royalist forces took advantage of insurgent hesitations and divisions within Indian society, waging counterinsurgent warfare with militia sent from the viceregal centers of Lima and Buenos Aires.

By late 1781, the core of the insurgency was broken, though scattered resistance and sporadic efforts to restart the movement persisted until

1784. Tupaj Katari, who had refused to surrender willingly, was put to death in a gruesome display of Spanish colonial justice. On 14 November 1781, at the Sanctuary of Peñas, his limbs were tied to the tails of four horses, and his body ripped apart as steeds careened off in different directions. The severed limbs of his corpse were then put on display in provincial capitals throughout the realm to warn the populace against future insubordination.

Repercussions

The importance of the Andean insurrection of 1780–1 was not lost on anyone, yet different groups drew radically different conclusions from the experience. Indians had seen the defeat of their own best hope for political hegemony in the Andes. The scope of their vision for self-rule now reduced down to the sphere of community autonomy. When creoles moved to break with peninsular Spanish control and establish their own autonomy in the early nineteenth century, and when royalist forces sought to put down this new challenge to colonial domination, Indian forces mobilized behind one side or the other, either under coercion or pragmatically, according to shifting military circumstances.

The lessons of 1780–1 for creoles were more ambiguous. On one hand, they had witnessed the impressive force of Indian mobilization and had every reason to fear and avoid the prospect of unleashing it in the future. The polarization in the latter stages of the conflict had dramatized for Spanish American elites the ancient fear of "caste war." Yet only a few decades after the great insurrection, beginning in 1809, a radical minority could draw a distinct conclusion: metropolitan control was vulnerable and Indian initiative insufficient to resolve the issue on its own. Creoles occupied a strategic position in colonial society, and by assuming leadership themselves, they would be able to direct restive social forces so as to achieve greater political representation and autonomy for American colonists and, ostensibly, for colonized Indian subjects.

Thus the first of the wave of independence movements to sweep Latin America in the early nineteenth century emerged in Upper Peru in 1809. In the wake of Napoleon's invasion of the Iberian Peninsula in 1807, and Fernando VII's abdication of the throne, political sovereignty dissolved in Spain, and fissures between American-born creoles and their peninsular counterparts opened up among Spanish elites in the New World. In the city of La Paz, a nucleus of creole radicals headed by Pedro Domingo Murillo made a bid for self-government given the vacancy of the crown. Their newly-constituted authority, the *Junta Tuitiva*, sounded an early proclamation of American autonomy: "Compatriots: Until now we have tolerated a sort of exile within the breast of our own country. We have looked on with indifference for more than three centuries as our primitive liberty was subject to the despotism and tyranny of an unjust usurper who, degrading us among mankind, has looked upon us as slaves; we have kept a silence closely resembling stupidity."[10] Although mainly an urban network, the conspirators recruited a limited number of *caciques* into their ranks and eventually raised a small army before royalist troops sent in from Cuzco stamped out the movement in November of 1809.

In 1811, the mestizo leader Juan Manuel Cáceres from La Paz—a member of the *Junta Tuitiva* now hailed as the General Restorer of the Indians of Peru—mounted a new campaign to cast off peninsular control. This led to Aymara community mobilizations throughout in the La Paz-Oruro-Cochabamba triangle, and a new siege of the city of La Paz from August to October. Not until early 1812 would arriving royalist troops mop up the last resistance.[11]

The rigidity of royalist rule eventually pushed liberal creoles defending their American homeland (*la patria*) in more overtly separatist directions. In 1814, a creole rebel movement in Cuzco placed the powerful *cacique* Mateo Pumacahua at its head. Pumacahua had earned royal favor decades earlier when he led his own Indian followers into battle against the forces of Tupaj Amaru, and again more recently in suppressing the outbreaks of insurgency in La Paz. Yet frustration at his own political marginalization now led him to break ranks with the crown. His armed movement in southern Peru, estimated at 20,000 troops, spilled over into the highlands of La Paz. Indian communities mobilized once again, and La Paz was the site of a new bloodbath, before they sputtered out in the face of counter-insurgency in early 1815. For the most part, highland *caciques* remained loyal to the crown in this period, leading their community members into battle to restore the status quo ante.

During the early to mid-1810s, creole troops from the newly-founded republic of Argentina and royalist armies from Lower Peru made periodic incursions into Upper Peru. They mustered rural support at times yet also provoked resentment due to their depredations, and hence they failed to gain lasting control over the territory. Meanwhile a cluster of six small rural zones, the patriotic *republiquetas*, sustained internal guerrilla resistance against royalist forces, again with some Indian community backing.

By 1816, however, crown forces under Viceroy Joaquín de la Pezuela held sway in most of the territory and a military showdown would have to wait until Simón Bolívar's republican armies arrived from the northern Andes. After the victory at Ayacucho in the central highlands of Peru in December 1824 expunged remaining resistance in Lower Peru, José de Sucre finally marched into Upper Peru to subdue the continent's last royalist stronghold in January 1825. Ironically, Latin America's first region to make a bid for autonomy in 1809 was the last to come to independence.[12]

"Bolivia" thus came into being out of an internecine war among European and American-born Spaniards. Significant changes resulted—the transition from monarchical to republican government prominent among them—yet not through the direct intervention of subordinate indigenous and plebeian sectors seeking to determine the contours of a new political and economic order. It was instead creole elites who accomplished in 1825 what Indian leaders had failed to achieve in 1780–1: an end to foreign domination and the expulsion of the metropolitan overlords. Tupaj Amaru had imagined that Indians, creoles, mestizos, and blacks would "live together like brothers and congregated in a single body," but under Indian political hegemony. Now creole liberators sought to incorporate subordinate Indians under enlightened white hegemony.

Drawing on liberal republican principles, creoles designed a new post-independence state with the ostensible purpose of amending the backward and benighted conditions of colonialism. Yet neither the older rifts between colony and metropole nor the recent years of military mobilization provided a unified sense of national self-consciousness or a coherent political bloc involving the Indian majority. Weak regional integration and flagging mining production as well as the reconstitution of racial/class hierarchy would lead to a renewal of colonial institutions and a creole "domination without hegemony."[13] Some two-thirds of the population was denied formal citizenship under the republican constitution, and

Indian tribute was restored to its status as the prime source of state revenue. At the time of its founding, the new nation's standard was planted in deep colonial soil.

4

Alliance and Repression in the Tributary Republic, 1826–1926

Having vanquished opponents from his native Venezuela down through the southern Andes to the country named after him, Simón Bolívar's initial decrees in 1824 and 1825 abolished Indian tribute, personal services to local notables, and the *mita* (mining labor draft imposed by the colonial state). Bolívar also sought to break up communal landholding and dissolve the indigenous community as a corporate entity. These were intended as progressive historical strokes that would sunder Americans' ties to the colonial past and clear the way for "modern" political institutions and public life, conceived according to a Northern Atlantic liberal blueprint.

Bolivian liberalism in the nineteenth century has been described as ethnocidal since it aimed to turn "Indians" into "Bolivians," without granting them the rights and status of "citizens." Land worked, held, and governed collectively—the very basis of Indian community life under Spanish colonialism—was to be converted into alienable private property. Indian community members would become individual patriarchal small-holders. If the sword of liberalism were to slice through the encrusted layers of the old regime, it had also to hack away—in order to liberate—Indian society itself.[1]

Liberalism in the Andes was fraught with contradiction, however, and the early bids for political and economic reform were ambivalent, tentative and quickly reversed. The "Liberator" himself, Simón Bolívar, spurned the egalitarian promise of political liberalism and deemed democracy a threat to social order: "If the principles of liberty are too rapidly introduced, anarchy and the destruction of the white inhabitants will be the inevitable consequences."[2] This fear was the lasting effect of Indian revolution in the Andes in the 1780s, slave revolution in Saint-Domingue (Haiti) in the 1790s and early 1800s, and the threat to creole command that *pardo* (colored or mixed race) armies presented in Bolívar's own Venezuela. Neither liberals nor conservatives in Bolivia wanted effective democratic participation of the majority, either. Unlike the anti-colonial model of interethnic brotherhood and political co-participation conceived during the eighteenth-century Andean insurgencies, Bolivian liberalism settled on a formula of nationality without citizenship for the popular majority, until an imaginary future point when the lower (Indian) castes would be prepared to share the rights and benefits of civilization.

The tenets of economic liberalism first tried out in the 1820s, and again beginning in the 1870s, met with major obstacles as well. First and foremost was the state's own rickety fiscal condition. Until the 1880s, when taxes on mining and commerce began to provide a new basis for national budgets, successive Bolivian governments depended primarily on revenue from tribute, hence on the existence of landholding Indian communities on a massive scale. This was unlike Colombia, Peru, and Ecuador, where Indian tribute was abolished mid-century and large agrarian estates grew rapidly.

But even as the combined pressures of state and market increased in the countryside, liberalism ran up against communal resistance to land privatization at the local level. Intra-elite disputes over appropriation of the surplus produced by the laboring classes and over control of the state also created sporadic political instability. While normally excluded from formal political participation, Indians were occasionally sought out for alliances to resolve such factional clashes. These alliances with dissident or displaced sectors of the creole ruling establishment were short-lived—emerging in the late 1860s, at points in the 1880s and 1890s, and again starting in the 1910s—and ended badly. Yet they could provide the context for autonomous political projects such as that of Pablo Zárate Villca and the network of Indian leaders known as the *cacique-apoderados*.[3]

Internal Colonialism Instated

In 1826, Indians constituted some 800,000 out of a population of 1,100,000, and 90 percent of all people living in the territory of the new nation-state lived in the countryside. The white or creole population,

estimated at only 200,000, enjoyed the benefits of the greatest property
wealth, income through commerce or professional salaries, and education—the very advantages that would be required for citizenship. At the
same time, oligarchic elites tended to be fragmented along regional lines,
and national integration was impeded by the rigorous mountain geography
and the rough conditions of the road system. The highland Andean region
of La Paz was home to the largest city in the country, with a population
of 40,000, over half of it Aymara. The highland valleys of Cochabamba,
with their Quechua-speaking peasantry, were the main site of the colonial
hacienda sector. Chuquisaca to the southeast was the old political capital,
linked to the silver circuit of Potosí. The vast Amazonian lowlands in the
east were largely unsettled, beyond the Spanish city of Santa Cruz de la
Sierra. The new administrative divisions of Bolivia—its cantons, provinces,
and departments—were modeled on those of Napoleonic France.

The decline of the silver mining sector from the 1790s through the
1820s, the limits to agricultural and manufacturing enterprise, and the
hostility of the upper classes to paying a property and income tax left
the new government without income. Marshal Antonio José de Sucre,
Bolivia's first president and Bolívar's closest collaborator, was quickly forced
to repeal Bolívar's ban on tribute in July 1826, thus renewing the close
colonial relationship between state fiscal needs, tributary extraction, and
non-liberal forms of community life.

In 1831, President Andrés de Santa Cruz (1829–39)—another bold
reformer and statesman, as well as a military hero like his predecessor,
Sucre—declared Indians the owners of all lands they had occupied for
more than ten years, in a new attempt to foment an individualized property
regime. But in 1842, President José Ballivián (1841–7) reverted to the
former policy of the Spanish crown, declaring Indian lands to be state
property held only in usufruct by Indian communities in exchange for a
contribution to the state. The chronically weak central state was incapable
of enforcing Ballivián's decree in any event, so it remained a dead letter;
the Indians were thus the de facto owners of most of the land in the
western highlands and highland valleys. The disorganized, cash-poor
government that emerged in the 1830s and 1840s hinged on the perpet-
uation of colonial relations of surplus extraction through tribute, not
privatization or state ownership of Indian community lands.

Through the monopoly on formal political participation and in the absence of political parties, tiny oligarchic factions, miniscule middle sectors, and artisans fought over control of the state through alliances with *caudillos*. These were usually military strongmen of humble or middling origins who had risen politically during or after the wars of independence. While *caudillo* bosses were central to shifting political coalitions from the 1840s to 1870s, centrifugal regional and local forces meant that once obtained, central government administration yielded limited results for the victors.[4]

In much of the highlands, the *hacienda* sector—composed of large agrarian estates partly integrated into regional markets and relying on servile labor—was dwarfed in demographic terms by Indian communities. In Cochabamba, the main breadbasket for the altiplano mining centers of Potosí and Oruro since the early colonial period, entrepreneurial peasant smallholders eroded landlord control over production and marketing. Throughout the early republican period in the 1830s and '40s, communities and independent smallholders engendered a dynamic, transnational network of peasant markets dependent on long-distance llama- and mule-drivers (*arrieros*), who linked northern Argentina, northern Chile, and southern Peru—zones of indigenous predominance—with Bolivia. In northern Potosí, Indian communities of Chayanta, for example, marketed wheat to nearby highland mining and commercial centers, while *arrieros* opened markets in forage crops along their routes.[5] Credit for this thriving peasant economy was also in the hands of wealthy indigenous people, who had to fulfill communal obligations in order to retain rights to land, as opposed to creoles or mestizos with no such obligations.[6] Thus community norms of moral economy and collective discipline placed limits on accumulation by rich indigenous peasants, who did not emerge as a distinct class within Indian communities in this period.

This popular economy and society was gradually targeted for liquidation after mid-century by oligarchic "modernizers." During the Age of Capital (1848–75), Anglo-Chilean capital investment in silver mining technology, infrastructure, and transport surged, as Bolivia re-entered the world capitalist market under the leadership of the aristocratic merchant-landlord-mining entrepreneurs known as the "patriarchs of silver": Aniceto Arce, Mariano Baptista and Gregorio Pacheco, each of whom would become president in the late nineteenth century. In conjunction with foreign capital, these mine owners were able to represent their business interests via direct control of the central government. They were based in the southern region of Chuquisaca, where the former administrative seat of the Spanish colonial district of Charcas continued as capital of the republic under its new name, Sucre.[7]

After the initial failures of Bolivarian decree, President Mariano Melgarejo launched the first serious onslaught against Indian community landholding after 1868. Melgarejo, the quintessential "barbarous *caudillo*" who hailed from a small Cochabamba town and seized power through military coup in 1864, did not act out of liberal ideological conviction and was resented by the "civilized" caste and opponents he had displaced politically. In 1870, rival *caudillos* in La Paz mobilized the Aymara communities of the high plains to overthrow Melgarejo. Once again, as in 1781 and 1811, the city of La Paz came under siege and the military dictator was forced to flee for his life to Peru. In the aftermath of the uprising, stolen community lands, monopolized by the Melgarejo clan and its friends, clients, and retainers, were mainly returned to Indian communities. This demonstrated the effectiveness of Indian community insurgency in determining the results of armed, intra-oligarchic conflict, as well as the political importance of creole-Indian community alliances.[8]

In the second silver cycle of the 1870s and '80s, Anglo-Chilean capital figured ever more prominently in the development of the mining industry centered near Sucre and Potosí, and ambitious railroad projects linking Bolivian mines to the Pacific coast were envisioned. The Anglo-Chilean business associates of the "patriarchs of silver" also had their eye on the rich nitrate reserves, sought after as fertilizer for exhausted agricultural soils back in England, in the coastal desert region of Atacama. They would be the principal beneficiaries of the brutal and lopsided "War of the Pacific" (1879–80), when Chile invaded Bolivian and Peruvian territory and permanently annexed Bolivia's coastline. This conflict would leave an open wound in Bolivia's national psyche and enduring resentment of its neighbor.

The trauma of external defeat and the unruliness of internal *caudillo* feuding caused political elites to close ranks. They institutionalized a more stable political order, based on political parties, in 1880. The oligarchic, bi-partisan political system of Liberals and Conservatives installed under General Narciso Campero also served to exclude popular—particularly Indian peasant—participation in politics.

Ascendant Liberalism

By the 1870s, with the rising fortunes of silver mining and the decreasing dependence of state budgets on tribute, a ruling-class consensus emerged over the need to deal with the "Indian question" via the break-up of Indian communities and sale of community lands. Seventy percent of Bolivia's 1,400,000 inhabitants were still indigenous at the time.[9] The 1874 "Disentailment Law" threatened the continued existence of Indian communities by subjecting land and natural resources held in common to privatization and sale, following liberal economic doctrine. Yet given the lack of national unity among regionally-based, property-owning creole miners and merchants, and the threat of Indian resistance, no government had the power to put the law into practice.

In 1881, land surveyors (*revisitadores*) were sent out to fix boundaries and put up for sale purportedly vacant community lands. The catalyst for this was the state's need to raise revenue to pay off war debts, and the effect was to turn the "Disentailment Law," promulgated yet not applied in 1874, into a new spatial reality in which private property would predominate. It also provided an opening for land-grabbing by local townspeople and land-lords through fraud and coercion. The land surveys generated immediate and widespread community resistance, however, as Indians massed to block the entrance of surveyors into community territory.[10]

This form of direct action forced the passage of a law in 1883 that allowed communities to claim lands on the basis of colonial titles. An "invented tradition" of leadership formed in the 1880s and '90s: commu-nities selected indigenous leaders (*apoderados*) to represent them before the courts and regional and local government, and many did so claiming hereditary descent from ethnic leaders from the colonial period (*caciques*).[11] These representatives formed a loosely coordinated, national network—the eastern lowlands were as yet sparsely inhabited, and largely cut off from the western highland and highland valley economy—of *cacique-apoderados* dedicated to blocking or reversing dispossession and combating the collusion of local officials and land surveyors with aspiring landlords.[12] By the late 1880s, Indian leaders petitioned President Aniceto Arce on behalf of their communities, complaining of the rigidity and disdain of local and regional Conservative officials, and of the ineffectiveness of legal forms of redress. Despite their pressures and pleas, one third of community lands would pass into private hands in the 1880s, most of them in the department of La Paz.[13] They described their situation as follows: "This is how much the prefects, sub-prefects, and other subaltern officials in town and country misunderstand us: they look on us with tedium, our legal petitions subject to oblivion . . . looking at us as beings of a different type, and very similar to savage beasts."[14]

Indian peasant communities were not the only group excluded from the benefits of the new order. After the introduction of the bi-party system in 1880, Conservatives monopolized elections, and hence the regional and local administrative offices of prefect, sub-prefect, *corregidor*, and land surveyor. This meant that Liberals were forced outside the boundaries of the system they helped design in order to make a place for themselves within it. As early as 1884, disaffected Liberals, convinced it would be impossible to take power by electoral means, began making alliances with the network of Indian community leaders.[15] Rebel caudillos in 1870 had shown the way to take power, and Liberals—based in La Paz like the earlier opponents of Melgarejo—promised the Indian communities return of their stolen lands.

There were other underlying regional and economic antagonisms at work as well. The Conservative Party was linked to entrenched oligarchic interests, especially the traditional silver mining and banking sectors in the southern regions of Chuquisaca and Potosí. The Liberal Party, on the other hand, reflected the interests of rising elites in the northern regions of La Paz and Oruro. Elites in La Paz had developed diversified investment strategies that included control over Indian community land and labor power, but they were tied especially to the new tin-mining industry—a distinct, northern commodity circuit of import-export business connected to the Pacific. The region of Oruro had been integrated in a subordinate role within the silver circuit centered on Sucre in the 1850s, and had seen a century of declining fortunes in its own silver mines. But the small city of Oruro was at the crossroads of capitalist development in Bolivia with the arrival of the railroad from Antofagosta, Chile, in 1892.

Fortunes tied to silver declined precipitously once the gold standard was adopted in the 1890s, making control over central government purse-strings that much more important for the maintenance of Conservative power. Merchant-miner-landlords from La Paz complained, not without reason, that their contribution to the national budget dwarfed that of other departments. They demanded a larger portion of state allocations. But given the balance of political forces, dominated by representatives of the silver circuit, tax monies stayed in Sucre. It was against this "centralist despotism" that federalist rebellion began to brew.

After 1895, a federalist project for regional autonomy achieved coherence among the propertied in the north, and Oruro played a key role in articulating it. Wealthy merchant-miners, who fused with and married into powerful elite circles in La Paz, found their ideologue in Adolfo Mier, an *orureño*. Mier stressed the impossibility of governing a country as diverse and heterogeneous as Bolivia from the center, given the strength of local customs and practices.[16] Oruro was also a convenient point of convergence for Indian leaders from parts of La Paz, Cochabamba, and Potosí.

To overthrow Conservatives, Liberals would follow the pattern set in the La Paz region in 1870 by uniting with aggrieved highland Indian communities. When Conservative Severo Fernández Alonso became president via fraudulent elections in 1896, five thousand Indian community members gathered on the rim of El Alto, shouting "Tata Pando"—Father Pando—down into the canyon of the city to strike fear into Conservative supporters of Alonso. The Liberal candidate, Senator José Manuel Pando, an adventurer-explorer who had run for president at the behest of notables in La Paz, had also participated in the overthrow of Melgarejo in 1870, through which stolen community lands had been returned. At the end of the nineteenth century, insurgent Aymara communities cast Pando as a father-protector in whose name they were soon to mobilize on a vast scale.

Civil War or Race War?

The Federal War began in late December 1898 when *paceño* elites, quickly followed by counterparts in Oruro, declared themselves in revolt against *chuquisaqueño* centralism and then recruited Aymara communities to beat back President Alonso's advance on La Paz. The Federal Army, led by Colonel-cum-General Pando, delegated military authority to one of his closest allies, Pablo Zárate "Villca," and Villca, in turn, delegated authority to local-regional *caciques* who mobilized the communities of the southern altiplano and highland valleys into an insurgency larger than anything seen since 1781. The insurgencies represented an ethnic confederation of

indigenous authorities and territories that covered much of Oruro, southern La Paz, western Cochabamba, and northern Potosí.

Though smaller in scope than the anti-colonial insurgencies in the late
eighteenth century, Indian self-government was extensive enough to point
to a new configuration of power and territory, in which Indian community
authorities would have a political and military place in the republic. The
federalism advocated by Liberal intellectuals, party leaders, and their
provincial political brokers—which promised to return stolen community
lands, as in 1870, and an end to colonial tribute exactions—seems to
have meshed with older Aymara community ideas of collective control
over land tenure, natural resources, and local and regional self-government,
as well as exceptional anti-colonial practices of refusal to pay tribute.

These ideas found expression in insurgent federalist governments of
1899, explicitly aligned with Pando and Villca in southern Oruro (Peñas,
Huancani, Hurmiri), northern Potosí (Sacaca), and southern La Paz
(Mohoza). In Mohoza, an insurgent government was led by "President"
Lorenzo Ramírez; in Sacaca, by "President" Mauricio Pedro; in Peñas,
by "President" Juan Lero. Along with Villca, Lero and Ramírez had signed
the above-mentioned letter to then-President Arce complaining of the
lawlessness of local officials—a full decade before leading Aymara troops
in support of Liberals in the Federal War.

Now communities in the Aymara heartland began to govern according
to their own law. Alongside "President" Lero in Peñas, for example,
Manuel Flores served as "Secretary," Feliciano Mamani as "Police Inten-
dant," Ascencio Fuentes as "Rigorous Judge/*Corregidor*," and Gregorio
Chaparro as "Colonel," among others. Thus, the alliance with Liberals
did not prevent or contradict the spread of indigenous self-rule, and may
have been its condition of possibility.

A turning point occurred when Indians in the canton of Mohoza, located
in southern La Paz near the Oruro border, rose up and attacked Liberal
troops, their ostensible allies, because of local abuses by the soldiers in February
1899. Pando wrote to his adversary, "No one is unaware of the evils that
this internal war is causing; to these one can add, as an inevitable result, 'race
war', which now comes from the impulse of the indigenous race."[17]

For local elites, state functionaries, and criminal prosecutors, the massacre
at Mohoza brought back memories of Tupaj Amaru. Yet in their vision,
Indians' initial pursuit of interethnic alliance in 1780–1 had been erased,

along with the recent memory of Pando's triumphant arrival in Oruro in mid-April 1899, with "President" Lorenzo Ramírez and Ramírez's Indian peasant irregulars from Mohoza at his side. The interethnic alliance—nicely symbolized by Ramírez and Pando celebrating victory together—that Indians tried to uphold even as they formed wartime governments of their own making broke down over the issue of Indian self-government, which was officially cast as "race war." In Mohoza, the attack on marauding Liberal troops had in fact resulted from confusion over whether they were Conservative "*alonsistas*" (a reference to followers of Conservative President Alonso) trying to pass themselves off as Liberal allies of Pando.

Readings that follow Pando and the prosecutors by casting the 1899 insurgencies as "race war"—or an archaic "*jaquerie andienne*"—have dominated historiography, but they miss the contest for property, labor, and political power that unfolded within Aymara communities. Indians who identified themselves as "merchants and property owners," or "town residents," were considered linked to Conservative elites in the cantons and vice-cantons. Communities defined their enemies as "*alonsistas*," the "rich," "property owners," and those "in contact" with *hacendados*. However, there was no mention of killing all "whites and mestizos."

In southern Oruro and northern Potosí, insurgent violence highlighted growing class differentiation in Indian peasant communities. This had resulted from the rapid growth of the land market in areas near the new rail line, like Challapata. Indians whose conduct violated community norms of moral economy and threatened its reproduction from within as well as those who had threatened to organize the counterinsurgency were the first to be subject to ritual sacrifice. Though local landlords and state officials were aware that the violence was political and erupting within Indian society, its significance was overlooked because it did not fit with the official script of "race war."

Insurgent violence was also selective, political, and informed by Andean cultural expectations when directed against state officials. According to "Colonel" Gregorio Chaparro, "President" Juan Lero's most powerful lieutenant in Peñas (Oruro), when insurgents targeted the *Corregidor* Celestino Vargas for sacrifice, they believed his "law" and his "time" had expired. This anticipation of an epochal political transformation resembled the historical consciousness of eighteenth-century Andean insurgents who had challenged colonial domination in the belief that "the present was another time."[18]

However, it was Chaparro's law and time that did not last, as he was sentenced to death and perished along with fellow insurgents who fought for Pando and Villca under the command of President Juan Lero. Lero defended himself by refusing the terms of his accuser:

> Since the dawn of my life, my heart has cultivated healthy principles, inculcating respect for life, honoring property, and condemning crimes and abuses. I find myself accused of multiple murders . . . The calumny to which humans are prone submerges me in pain, but with my head serene and my conscience clear, I await the results of justice, though I do not ask for pardon because I do not need it. I need the correct application of the law.[19]

At sixty, Lero died in prison of chronic dysentery before the executions began, but on the basis of communal codes of law and justice, he had disputed the lawlessness of the liberal republic. Villca's fate was equally tragic—he was shot while being transferred from Oruro to La Paz—and his defense, spoken in Spanish without the aid of an interpreter, was no less eloquent:

> As one of the chief auxiliaries of the army, facing off against the Constitutionalists with the means of destruction at their disposal, I could have been exterminated, which would have been better given the prison and trials to which I am subject for having sacrificed myself for the country. I am not learned enough to go around vaingloriously trumpeting the positive services I have given for the triumph of republican institutions in the Bolivian homeland (*patria*) . . . As much as anyone, I respect everyone's right to property as well as life.[20]

More than ten years before being put on trial, both Villca and Lero had been signatories of the letter to then-President Arce that had complained of the inhumanity of local officials. At the end of their lives, both insisted that extermination of whites had *not* been the shared aim of insurgents; rather, both emphasized their own humane commitments to building a more just, more equitable country—indeed, theirs was a radical leveling.

Community insurgency in the Federal War was based on political, cultural, and spiritual codes that combined pre-colonial forms of ritual warfare, claims for early- and mid-colonial precedents regarding land tenure, invented "neocolonial" traditions of "noble" lineage for community leaders, and late-colonial democratic controls over leadership and aspirations to end tributary extraction. Republican political-military elements—the offices of President, General, Colonel—were added to the repertoire, along with federalist ideas. All of this underscores the extraordinary, and hitherto largely unrecognized, creativity of Indian community politics in the oligarchic republic.

Insurgents sought not the extermination of creoles and mestizos, but local and regional autonomy based on Indian community hegemony in the countryside. This project came into view in the western high plains, mountain tops, and highland valleys in 1899, but it was quickly snuffed out when Liberals abandoned their erstwhile Indian allies and re-negotiated power with Conservatives.[21] Indelibly stained with the mark of Aymara insurgency, federalism was jettisoned as soon as Liberals came to power in a re-constituted oligarchic republic.

Liberal Order

If elite consensus was to be forged in the aftermath of civil war, alternative indigenous projects based on political autonomy, self-government, and collective land use within the republic had to be made unthinkable through repression, discursive as well as practical. In well-publicized trials against rebels from Peñas (1899–1901) and Mohoza (1901–4), Aymara communities were cast as savage, bloodthirsty descendants of Tupaj Amaru, motivated by an "insatiable thirst for revenge," who aimed to overturn the republican order.

Victorious thanks to Aymara community insurgency, and then in the aftermath of successful repression, Liberal elites became the first centralizing nation-builders in republican history, self-consciously trying to overcome an aristocratic, colonial legacy of regional fragmentation. Members of the Geographic Society of La Paz and veteran commanders of the Federal War, Bolivian presidents Pando (1899–1904) and Ismael Montes (1904–9; 1913–17) helped to map and quantify natural resources and population and to develop transportation networks so as to facilitate commercial exploitation of raw materials, labor power, and territory. "The geographic period," borrowing Pando's own celebratory phrase for the state projects undertaken, was also a time of reconsolidation of the agrarian property regime.

Yet in the early years of the new century, Liberal elites failed to achieve hegemony or bring into being the modern nation of their imagination. Their attempt to form a "national space," radiating out from La Paz, did not actually eliminate the "seigneurial space" of the hacienda and mining enclaves.[22] With a landlord offensive against communities, especially in the densely-populated Lake Titicaca region, Liberal nation-builders used the law, the courts, and the press to bury insurgent community federalism underground, and turned land into a commodity—one that came with dependent labor services attached—to an extent not yet seen in Bolivia. It is no accident that Pando and Montes became two of the largest landlords in the Liberal republic.[23]

The growth of the mining industry had weaned the state of its dependence on Indian tribute and allowed for the liberal land legislation at the end of the nineteenth century. But the actual result was a "neofeudal" agrarian structure based on established modes of colonial extraction and exploitation in the countryside. The large landed estate emerged as the dominant form of property and production in the twentieth century, not before.[24]

Liberals had betrayed, then crushed their Indian allies in the name of civilization and national consensus, but like Conservatives after 1880, they ended up denying other factions of the elite a share of power. By the time World War I began, former Conservatives and breakaway sectors of the Liberal Party, as well as a new layer of middle-class professionals, repeated the pattern established by Liberals in the 1880s and '90s. They organized the Republican Party to contest elections, plot coup attempts (*golpes de estado*), and develop ties with restive popular sectors.

Though led by elites that Liberals excluded from exercising formal political power, the Republican Party was popular in composition as a result of its alliances with high-plains Aymara communities and artisans in the cities. In 1914, the so-called Pacajes revolt began in the mining center of Corocoro, and spread to the provinces of Pacajes, Aroma, Loayza, Ingavi, and Los Andes in the department of La Paz. At its head, "Great *Cacique*" Martín Vásquez counted on Republican allies like the Monroy brothers, lawyers who accompanied Vásquez on his first trip to Lima where they unearthed colonial land titles from Peruvian archives for use in Bolivian courts. In the 1914 revolt, the *corregidor* was ritually sacrificed, as in 1899, and insurgent communities demanded control over local and regional office along with recovery of stolen community lands. Since the Pacajes uprising did not spread to other departments, it was quickly squelched. Yet until 1920, despite being in and out of prison, Martín Vásquez and Santos Marka T'ula, who assumed the mantle of *cacique* of Callapa (La Paz), broadened their network of regional-local leaders dedicated to reversing a liberal dynamic that led to forced land sales and feudal labor services. Violence and extra-economic coercion prevailed.

Through the alliances formed in cantons and vice-cantons, the network of *cacique-apoderados* shaped the unfolding of the Republican coup in 1920, with Aymara communities in the Titicaca region mobilizing on behalf of the Republican cause:

> Indians allied with them. They were praised: "The Republican is on the side of the Indian, the Liberal no. Liberals are landlords." And it was true . . . That's why we said, "They are on the side of the Indians." The workers and others voted for them. The others, the rich, were from the Liberal Party.[25]

The victor in the coup of 1920 was Republican Party leader Bautista Saavedra, a lawyer, criminologist, ethnographer, and linguist, author of a study of the Andean community, and distinguished member of the Geographic Society of La Paz. Saavedra had defended Mohoza insurgents as a young lawyer from 1901–04, setting the terms of enlightened discourse on "the Indian question" for the Liberal republic. Landlords, *corregidores*, and priests, the local relics of the colonial order, had been largely to blame for community insurgency in 1899, because of their perverse exploitation of Indians. This triumvirate became known as the "three plagues" afflicting indigenous community life. Indians were assumed to be essentially irrational; normally passive yet at points excitable. What they needed, and what the nation needed to solve "the Indian question," was the moral and cultural leadership of enlightened creoles.[26]

In 1920, Saavedra had risen to power with the help of insurgent Aymara communities and their representatives, but when indigenous forces exerted more autonomous initiative after the Republican triumph, they suffered the type of repression endured by the previous generation after the Federal War of 1899. After a local revolt in Jesús de Machaqa (La Paz) in 1921, Saavedra made a volte-face and brutally cracked down. Now he no longer blamed landlords and local authorities for abuse, but unscrupulous local lawyers for agitating among the communities and stirring up those individuals who manipulated titles like "*cacique*" and "governor." Saavedra saw insurgency not simply as an ethnocidal project designed to exterminate white people in general, but rather as an effort to end the rule of private property from which whites had benefited. He also recognized the "desire of the aboriginal element to re-establish a confederated government ruled by autochthonous authorities"—insurgents had not only killed the acting *corregidor* but also allegedly nominated their own *corregidor*, mayor, governor, and priest. This was clearly threatening to the new president, and he insisted that state violence was necessary to guarantee the physical security of landlords, their property, and the established order.[27]

The Machaqa uprising was led by the Llanquis, Faustino and his son Marcelino, who had participated in Santos Marka T'ula's movement, which now included a project for indigenous education as well as local self-government and restoration of community lands.[28] In spite of the massacre of some fifty rebels in Machaqa, the southern wing of the network of *cacique-apoderados* redoubled its efforts to pit the central government against the "three plagues" in the countryside. Taking advantage of Saavedra's "Law of Indigenous Literacy," passed in 1923, they founded schools throughout the highlands and valleys despite the harassment of local officials and land-lords. Educating community leaders for the "liberation" of their communities went hand in hand with the goals of reclaiming community lands using colonial titles and exercising community control over local authorities. In pursuing these goals, the movement exposed the cracks in the oligarchic republic and chipped away at the brittle rule of miners-landlords-merchants.

5

National-Popular Stirrings, 1927–44

In the late nineteenth and early twentieth century, alliances between Indian peasant communities and creole elite conspirators helped determine the results of armed contests for control of the state. By 1927, the pattern changed: Indian community leaders made alliances not with dissident elites—as in the case of Liberals and Republicans earlier—but with emergent radical forces and labor movements on the left that had emerged during and after World War I, thus heralding the possibility of future national-popular political projects.

This was brought home with special force during the uprising in Chayanta in 1927. Chayanta was a carefully prepared and organized Indian community rebellion that had the support of radical urban allies. Like Tomás Katari's movement in the same region in the late eighteenth century, it sought to bring an end to a time of abuse and to introduce a new law and a new justice. Though it was not coordinated with mass actions by artisans and proletarians in the cities and though it lacked national scope, it was the largest community insurgency since 1899, and summoned up simultaneous agrarian insurrection in Sucre, Potosí, Oruro, and Cochabamba.

By the 1930s, the building momentum of a new cluster of political actors would alter the national scene. The network of *caciques-apoderados* kept up steady efforts defending the lands, communities, and rights of indigenous Bolivians. New revolutionary left and labor organizations were on the rise. And after the devastating crisis of the Chaco War (1932–5) against Paraguay, radical nationalism would surge among the laboring and middle classes as well as among sectors of the military. Ultimately this proliferation of radical popular and nationalist forces would pose an insurmountable threat to the seigneurial oligarchy.

The Chayanta Rebellion

When Hernando Siles of the Republican Party took office as president in 1926, an alliance had begun to mature in Sucre and Potosí between Indian *caciques*, radical lawyers, educators, artisans, and intellectuals in the new Socialist Party. The *caciques* counted on the support of the rector of the University of Chuquisaca who, according to Saavedra's 1923 Indian literacy law, was authorized to sanction the founding of schools. Radical lawyers linked to emergent anarcho-syndicalist trade unions and schools, like the one founded by Rómulo Chumacero in 1922 and named after the Spanish anarchist Francisco Ferrer y Guardia, began to work with Indian *caciques* like Manuel Michel, who had been elected "General *Cacique* of Sucre/Potosí" in a general assembly of his peers, and with Agustín Saavedra, Manuel Michel's "Commissioner of Education."

There had been earlier attempts in the 1920s to found a progressive and popular party independent of oligarchic influence, yet it was not until 1927 that the Socialist Party began to cohere as a radical force. The man who took center stage was Tristán Marof, the literary and political name of a native son of Sucre, Gustavo Navarro. Marof was a former radical Republican who became a Sorelian Marxist after World War I in Europe, where he occupied a series of consular posts from which he wrote novels and polemical pamphlets. He was also a comrade and collaborator of Peruvian Marxist José Carlos Mariátegui, and one of Marof's texts (*La justicia del Inca*, 1926) forecast Indian revolution in Bolivia.

In March 1927, when he was newly arrived from Europe, Marof invited "General *Cacique*" Manuel Michel and other local Indian community leaders to the Third National Workers' Congress in Oruro. Michel seized the opportunity to denounce exploitative local authorities: "I spoke out, making it known that we are subject to enormous abuses, and that officials do not protect us." The Congress issued resolutions warning local and regional officials of the potential consequences of inaction and authorizing the right to organize rural trade unions.[1] Manuel Michel joined the Socialist Party in early 1927, and Marof and the tailor Rómulo Chumacero directed a growing radical coalition in Sucre and Potosí.

In contrast to subsequent relations between Indian communities, left intellectuals and activists, and organized labor, what stands out about Socialist Party efforts to unite with the *caciques* in Sucre, Potosí, and Oruro, is that

Socialist militants recognized the demands for Indian community self-government and collective land use. They suggested that just as the "salvation" of workers would be the task of workers themselves, so the "liberation of the Indian will be the responsibility of the Indians themselves."[2] The workers' congress in Oruro was the first to demand the nationalization of the country's tin mines, campaign for women's rights and Indian literacy, and declare class struggle the means to achieve its demands. The call for "lands to the people and mines to the state"—first sounded in Marof's *La justicia del Inca*—was here proclaimed as an official slogan. At least in some aspects, the Congress prefigured a national-popular focus, but with a significant agrarian component, influenced by Indian *cacique* participation.

On 25 July 1927, a day of celebration dedicated to Santiago, the Catholic warrior and patron-saint of Spain, Indian communities and hacienda *colonos* (peons or tenants) rose up in Sucre, Potosí, Oruro, and Cochabamba.[3] Though planned in advance, witnesses declared that the immediate provocation for the revolt was the rape of a hacienda tenant and theft of six cows by the former prefect of Potosí, Nicanor Serrudo. Insurgents used fire—Santiago's symbol—as a weapon, and farmhouses and crops burned throughout the Indian heartlands in the highlands and highland valleys.

Insurgents killed the *corregidor* of Ocurí, in northern Potosí, subjected Serrudo to a self-organized judicial process which led to the expropriation of his lands, and ritually sacrificed another landlord and former public official before burying his bones on a sacred mountain top at Condor Nasa (4,645m). Rebels aimed to halt the advance of hacienda encroachment, retake stolen community lands, and punish landlords for rape, theft, and forced labor on their rural estates. Coercing local officials into signing trial proceedings and land titles over to communities, insurgents administered justice according to their law. By attacking the *corregidor* and replacing him with one appointed by the community, and ritually sacrificing someone who embodied the fusion of formal politics and the theft of communal lands, rebels aimed to end the reign of abusive local officials, private property, and to govern themselves at local and regional levels.

Leading up to and during the Chayanta rebellion, *caciques* and "*alcaldes de escuelas*" (secretaries of education) pressed for the implementation of official government and opposition decrees, reflecting their understanding of law and justice, continually petitioning and pressuring officials, from local *corregidores* to President Siles.[4] Thus insurgents did not discard legalism in favor of direct action, or exchange pacifism for violence. Like peasants elsewhere, they combined these seemingly contradictory tactics in a flexible political repertoire that had characterized community insurgency in Bolivia since the late eighteenth century. Earlier struggles were also kept alive or rekindled in memory and oral history, and helped inspire the *cacique-apoderado* movement in this period:

> "There have to be schools. We have to stop being slaves. They have to stop imprisoning us. In the ancient [land] titles it says that the Indian is free" . . . We found documents with that content . . . We also talked about Tupaj Katari: "Tupaj Katari rose up against the Spaniards, since the Spaniards wanted to eliminate Indians at any cost. That's why Tupaj Katari rose up against Spaniards, to defend himself, and that's why the Spaniards killed him," they said. "That's why we have to struggle."[5]

At home and abroad, though, the uprising was branded "communist," and seen to threaten mining capitalism and the railroads—what the *New York Times* described as "white man's civilization," which involved loans going into tens of millions of dollars from the US and Britain to Bolivia.[6] After World War I, US capital investment spread beyond the Caribbean and Central America to the Andes, and its dominance in the hemisphere grew apace. So did anti-communism.

In Bolivia, fears of spreading communism, though not altogether without foundation, were greatly exaggerated. The urban artisans, intellectuals, and lawyers from Sucre/Potosí who led the most radicalized group of a liberal trade union movement, called for urban insurrections in support of the indigenous "comrades" who had taken over much of the countryside in the western highland valleys. Yet the hoped-for response failed to materialize. The uprising did not spread to the crucial department of La Paz, where landlord power was most deeply rooted; nor did artisans and proletarians organize revolt in Sucre, Potosí, or Oruro. A movement confined to one region—an economically and politically declining one at that, as the outcome of the Federal War had proven—had little chance of overthrowing the national government and installing a new one. Furthermore, the weakness of the links between the Indian peasant rebels and the mass of artisans and workers in cities and mines meant that the state could use cities and towns as headquarters for military "pacification" campaigns waged in rural areas. In the face of simultaneous urban insurrections, the military would have been thinly stretched, making the planning of counterinsurgency in the countryside more difficult.

From the perspective of Indian community members, the rebellion was not a failure, however: President Siles amnestied 184 leaders in October 1927, and thereafter blocked hacienda expansion in the south. Without taking power, then, insurgent community members and *colonos* in the western highland valleys achieved part of their goals. This point must be balanced, however, with the sober assessment of the longer-term national process: "Still holding half the lands . . . in 1880, the communities were reduced to less than a third . . . by 1930."[7]

It is important to take note of the tight connections between Indian community leaders and their urban counterparts. When "*compañeros*" Chumacero, Marof, and several others were arrested for inciting the uprising, Manuel Michel wrote directly to President Siles:

> They have done nothing besides help us in our complaints against the multiple injustices of which we are victims. Like many others, fortunately, they have understood their duty to put themselves on the side of the indigenous race, and they do it disinterestedly, giving us good advice, indicating to us the authorities to whom we should direct our demands, taking an interest in our uplift, founded especially on the education we need. And we are convinced above all, most excellent Sir, that the authorities, landlords, and all literate people are tenaciously opposed to letting our children learn to read . . . The ignorance in which they maintain us is the origin of our enslavement and those who try to pull us out of it are people of justice; they are human.[8]

Clearly, the leaders of the new urban radicalism had gained the confidence and trust of their indigenous allies. These qualities have more often been missing in Indian community-urban left relations in the twentieth century, while friction, misunderstanding, and blatant racism have tended to prevail. But in moments of collaboration and respect like this one, the combined political force that was generated made a real impression, not least of all on the existing authorities.

The development of the alliance between indigenous peasant forces, their organic leaders, and the most radical currents within the labor movement, however, was subsequently forestalled by the state of siege declared by Siles in 1927, and the cooptation of some labor leaders by the overhauled Siles regime. Subsequent convergence between urban radicals and Indian *caciques* were fleeting and ad hoc, and did not lead to enduring forms of political articulation. Yet comparable alliances reappeared during the Chaco War and after the mid-1940s, contributing to the first national revolutionary cycle. Though such alliances did not last, they left their imprints on each subsequent cycle.

The oligarchic republic's foundations were as economically weak as they were politically contested. The country depended heavily on one commodity, tin, which had displaced silver in the 1890s. As a result, Bolivian exports were extremely vulnerable to external shocks in the world market. The price of tin collapsed in 1929, the boliviano ceased to be convertible currency in 1931, and President Daniel Salamanca (1931–4) suspended payment on the external debt, which was equal to close to 50 per cent of exports.

Salamanca was a Cochabamba landlord and rigid political boss of the old Liberal stripe who had founded his Genuine Republican Party in 1921 after a split with Bautista Saavedra. Now in the throes of the Depression, he tried to ram through a "Law of Social Defense" to forestall popular mobilization. Though the industrial tin-mining elite (known as *la rosca*)—composed chiefly of three firms: Aramayo, Hochschild, and Patiño—came through the economic crisis intact, the expanding middle class was devastated along with the working class and peasantry.

The Chaco War

Already in deep crisis, the Bolivian government broke off relations with Paraguay following a border skirmish in July 1931, and in 1932 Salamanca blundered his way into a disastrous conflict with the Paraguayan military. Simon Patiño, whose enterprises counted for 10 percent of the world tin market by the time World War II began, provided 78 percent of the 2.5 million pounds sterling that the oligarchy loaned the Bolivian government for the purchase of 5,000 lorries, tanks, aircraft, mortars, machine guns, and flame-throwers.

Because of its disastrous consequences, the Chaco War helped create an oppositional, national-popular horizon of thought and action that had previously been the outlook of a radical minority—as evidenced by the limits of the Chayanta Rebellion. Out of a population of 2,000,000, some 250,000 combatants from various regions, classes, and races/castes came together to fight under appalling conditions in the southeastern Chaco borderlands disputed with Paraguay. Many would never return. In just thirty-six months, 52,400 died—overwhelmingly from natural causes such as dehydration, dysentery, and hunger. Over 20,000 were captured, 10,000 deserted, and thousands of square kilometers of "national" territory were lost.

For those who fought and who lived through it, like future tin miners' union boss Juan Lechín Oquendo and future National Revolutionary Movement (MNR) leaders such as Víctor Paz Estenssoro, Hernán Siles Suazo (son of Hernando Siles), and Walter Guevara Arze, the experience was definitive. The nationalism that grew out of the Chaco fiasco was neither xenophobic nor anti-Paraguayan, though it was strongly inflected with anti-imperialist accents.[9] The government of President Daniel Salamanca had not only proven its incompetence and contempt for the people, according to radical nationalists; in their masculinist terms, Bolivia's honor had been betrayed, and the country lay prostrate before the imperial concerns of Royal Dutch Shell—which, like the Argentine military, supported Paraguay—and Standard Oil, which supported Bolivia. The exclusive circle of politicians and professionals who ran the liberal state to suit the interests of the country's export elite would become the targets of a variegated but relentless nationalist invective—strongly influenced by national socialist ideology in its MNR and Bolivian Socialist Falange (FSB) manifestations.

This seigneurial oligarchy, especially identified with the "tin barons"— Patiño, the Aramayo family, and Mauricio Hochschild—was known as the *rosca* in popular parlance, and attacked as the anti-national tool of US imperialism. The press, including journalists with political aspirations, multiplied after the mid-1930s, as did sectarian divisions among middle-class aspirants to power. They also fought among themselves over the type of party to be created in opposition to the *rosca*. The intensity of middle-class political participation and the extent of its leadership represented something genuinely new in Bolivian politics.

There were, however, continuities as well. The Chaco War was a time of ongoing land conflict, unrest, and rebellion in the countryside, what one historian dubbed an "internal war."[10] This was particularly true in the department of La Paz, the region most deeply and adversely affected by merchant-landlord-miner rule under the liberal-style Republican governments of Bautista Saavedra, Hernando Siles, and Daniel Salamanca (1920–32). As the Chaco War began, and adult male Indian community members were sent to the front, landlords augmented their holdings through arbitrary land-seizures and fraud. Revolts then intensified toward the end of 1933 and, like Chayanta rebels, community insurgents were said to be influenced by revolutionary activists. Many creole militants on the left had been exiled to Argentina, Chile, or Peru, where they wrote anti-war pamphlets that were widely read and discussed in border areas and beyond.

Lacking more micro-level analyses, we cannot affirm that radical alliances between self-styled "revolutionaries" and insurgent communities, as in Chayanta, were reborn in the Chaco War. But throughout the La Paz countryside, in alliance with *colono* residents on haciendas, and allegedly working in concert with "communists," Aymara communities staged land takeovers and assaulted the persons and property of landlords.[11] The aging leader Santos Marka T'ula led the uprisings in the town of Guaqui, near Lake Titicaca, and established a national network of collaborators.

One of them, the tireless Indian activist Eduardo L. Nina Quispe, founded the Society of the "Republic of Collasuyu." Recalling the old Inka term for the territory now named Bolivia, his public association worked for Indian land rights and schools as part of a project for national regeneration. Like Tupaj Amaru and Aymara communities in the eighteenth century, he also possessed an ample vision of potential multi-ethnic coexistence: "All of us Bolivians obey in order to conserve liberty. The Aymara and Quechua languages are spoken by the indigenous race. Spanish is spoken by the white and mestizo races. All are our brothers." Yet Nina Quispe's advocacy led to charges of "communism," and for declaring himself President of the "Republic of Collasuyu" he was accused of attempting to supplant the constitutional authority of President Salamanca. Tried and convicted by a military tribunal in 1933, he was imprisoned for nearly three years.[12]

The community-*colono* insurgencies spread from La Paz to Oruro, Potosí, and Sucre in 1934, but were put down by the time the Chaco War concluded in 1935. After humiliating military losses and crude executive attempts to manipulate the military hierarchy, Salamanca was forced to resign by the army in late 1934. The following year, Bolivia and Paraguay fought to a standstill and both nations sought a solution to the draining war effort and tragic violence. The "internal war" between landlords and communities only subsided when the war against the external enemy finally came to an end.

"Military Socialism"

Nationalist interpretations signal the Chaco War as a rupture, a break with the rotten oligarchic order that led to the growth of new political parties and mass politics, premised on cross-class alliances and led by the educated, provincial middle classes. The key new parties were the Stalinist Institutional Revolutionary Party (PIR, 1940), the National Revolutionary Movement (MNR, 1941), the Trotskyist Revolutionary Workers' Party (POR, 1934), the fascist Bolivian Socialist Falange (FSB, 1941), and the Democratic Socialist Bolivian Socialist Workers' Party (PSOB, 1938). The Chaco War was also responsible for the rise of military men who were revolutionary nationalists such as Colonels David Toro (1936–7), Germán Busch (1937–9), and Gualberto Villaroel (1943–6).[13]

There were continuities between the 1920s and what came after. The Saavedra and Siles administrations (1920–9) combined the counter-insurgency of earlier Liberal regimes with new policies to court popular sectors, and in this they resembled the Revolutionary Nationalist Movement (MNR) and military authoritarianism after the 1950s. The radical positions of the Workers Congress and the Socialist Party went beyond the parameters of traditional oligarchic politics to anticipate national-popular dynamics after the Chaco War.[14] But changes that resulted from the Chaco War are as crucial as continuities. During the 1930s and '40s, Indian community insurgency was eclipsed as the leading current of resistance by the protagonism of increasingly radicalized miners, rural tenants, students, and the nationalist parties and regimes tied to them.

Defeat in the Chaco War and the structural crisis of the traditional political system brought about a decade of military governments. Colonels David Toro and Germán Busch were junior officers in the Chaco who became anti-oligarchic nationalists and partisans of so-called "military socialism," now that the elite parties and liberal caudillos were in disarray. With the support of Chaco veterans and organized labor, Toro introduced new social welfare legislation and the mandatory unionization of the work-force, a measure that would leave an important legacy for collective popular organization in the twentieth century—the trade union remains the basic form of organizing politics from below.

Toro's most radical step was the 1937 nationalization of Standard Oil, which had engaged in fraudulent business practices damaging to the fiscal interests of the Bolivian government. This was the first expropriation of a foreign company in twentieth-century Latin America—preceding Mexico's more ambitious nationalization of oil the next year. The most important development under Germán Busch was the 1938 national convention in La Paz which drafted a socially progressive new constitution overturning the orthodox liberal charter of 1880. At the convention, leftist delegates voiced radical new demands, inspired by Mexico's revolutionary constitution of 1917 and the ideas of Peruvian Marxist José Carlos Mariátegui. Though socialists were unable to dominate the convention, and the left was split between radicals and moderates, they left their stamp on the proceedings. The constitution of 1938 insisted on the "social func-tion" of property and outlined the state's role in guaranteeing public welfare and national economic interests.[15]

But if the period of military socialism was a fertile time for organized labor and the left, Indian peasant communities gained little. In national political debate, their interests were spoken for only indirectly, and by minority voices from the radical left. The progressive Labor Code passed under Busch in 1939 did not apply to agricultural workers, and the new constitution did not abolish hacienda servitude or redistribute agrarian property.

The Busch regime grew increasingly authoritarian and isolated, until the dictator took his own life in 1939. Amidst the collapse of the left-wing officer corps and factionalism on the civilian left, the conservative regimes of Generals Carlos Quintanilla (1939–40) and Enrique Peñaranda (1940–3) helped the *rosca* regroup temporarily. Standard Oil was indem-nified by the Bolivian government in 1942, and Busch's efforts to tax the *rosca* were repealed. But the "military socialists" had struck the first blows, and their efforts to ride the rising tide of popular forces would be imitated by middle-class leaders in the revolutionary period (1952–64), and by military leaders in the post-revolutionary period (1964–71). While the indigenous peasantry was marginalized in state politics, the nationalization of oil and the constitutional debates and reforms set a progressive foundation for future national-popular struggles.

6

Toward Revolution and Back, 1945–63

Rising Tides

Bolivia's second full-fledged revolutionary moment in 1952–3 was preceded by a new wave of popular unrest and a gradual breakdown of state power and ruling-class authority after the *rosca*'s restoration in the mid-1940s. In this phase, Indian and peasant insurgency in the countryside would coincide with proletarian activism, galvanized in the mining districts, to make possible deep changes in society. The struggles of the *cacique-apoderado* movement were sustained in this period, as Aymara and Quechua community members and *colonos* continued to challenge landlords over land, labor, and the right to education.[1]

Seeking to subdue the conflict in the countryside and to capture indigenous support, the military-nationalist government of Col. Gualberto Villarroel (1943–6) inaugurated the first National Indigenous Congress in 1945. Prior to the Congress, the "Bolivian Indigenous Committee," led by Luis Ramos Quevedo—a veteran rural organizer for Oruro's FOS (Workers' Trade Union Federation)—had drafted an extensive program that circulated in the national press. Like insurgents in 1899 or 1927, Quevedo and others in 1945 saw the land as "belonging to the Indians," and demanded it be "returned to the Community." By the time the Congress assembled, however, Ramos Quevedo had been jailed as an agitator and the official agenda, set by Villarroel's ministers and MNR allies, referred only to the sectoral problems of *colonos*, especially rural labor conditions and schooling. The official conclusions deliberately omitted any mention of the problems of land tenure and Indian peasant communities.

Despite its limitations, though, the Congress proved historic. This was the first time indigenous leaders could directly represent their own demands in a national political arena, and the first time any creole government decreed pro-active legislation on behalf of rural laborers. Most important was a ban on *pongueaje* and *mitanaje*, the unremunerated non-agricultural labor services supplied by male *pongos* and female *mitanis* for patriarchal landlords and their families.[2]

When landlords refused to heed the new laws, Indian community forces responded by linking legal recourse to direct action. Leaders sent in petitions denouncing abuses, and calling for rural education, land redistribution, and enforcement of the 1945 decrees. In 1946, sit-down strikes spread from the cantons of Mizque and Ayopaya throughout Cochabamba, and from there to northern Potosí. By 1947, there were widespread attacks on landlord power and property. In Ayopaya itself, *colonos* seized lands and communities appointed their own authorities to exercise local political power. While Ayopaya had only a small Indian community sector, the fact that *colonos* called for land to be returned to "the community" and for everyone to become "community members" suggests that the two sectors—*colonos* and *comunarios*—worked in tandem, there as elsewhere.

Indian peasant efforts in La Paz, Cochabamba, Potosí, Chuquisaca, and Tarija—excepting the former and the latter, the very departments involved in the Chayanta rebellion—culminated in a cycle of rural rebellion in 1946–7 that was the largest of the twentieth century. Reminiscent of the insurgent strategies and autonomist politics that undermined local state control in the eighteenth century, the rebellion contributed fundamentally to the revolutionary conjuncture of 1952–3.

In 1946, growing opposition to the abuses of the Villarroel regime led to the lynching of the president by an urban mob. When right-wing President Enrique Hertzog took power in 1947, he wasted no time in making good on threats he had issued in the press by mobilizing planes, the army, the national police, and the newly-minted rural police to massacre community and *colono* insurgents between January and June 1947. Leaders were arrested and sent to an agrarian labor camp in the Chapare lowlands. While the uprisings of 1946–7 were temporarily put down, the counter-insurgent *rosca* governments never succeeded in bringing the countryside under their jurisdiction. Landlords were steadily losing control; their law and their justice were unacceptable. Others had begun to be put in their place.[3]

The mobilization of 1946–7 also recalled the radical alliance of 1927. In fact, labor and left support for rural organizing had been renewed in the late 1930s. After the Chaco War, veterans began to form the country's first peasant unions in the Valle Alto of Cochabamba. The repercussions were felt throughout the northern altiplano. Aging leader Santos Marka T'ula began to adopt union sit-down strike tactics (*huelga de brazos caídos*) in organizing hacienda *colonos* in the Lake Titicaca region. In the 1940s, urban unions supported the first regional and national indigenous congresses, and Indian leaders came to join the anarchist Worker Federations as "Secretaries of Indigenous Affairs." During the rebel cycle of 1946–7, Esteban Quispe and Antonio Yucra, both members of the Local Workers Federation (FOL) of La Paz, led sit-down strikes of *colonos* on haciendas in the department of La Paz, demonstrating the links between trade unionism in the cities and land takeovers in the countryside. But whereas miners had played no appreciable role in 1927, by the 1940s their radicalizing impact on the rest of the proletariat was growing more palpable. For example, Gabriel Núñez, a miners' leader from Oruro, was in contact with Antonio Ramos, one of the leaders of the Ayopaya revolt.[4]

The political militancy and strength of mine workers were rising over the course of the 1940s in tandem with those of the left. The massacre of striking miners in Catavi in 1942 stirred protest and organization, and a congress held in the mining center of Huanuni two years later founded the Trade Union Federation of Bolivian Mine Workers (FSTMB). The miners' federation was instigated in no small part by the National Revolutionary Movement (MNR), a newly formed, center-left opposition party. Emerging out of post-Chaco War nationalist circles and attracted by European fascist trends, the MNR was led by middle-class intellectuals such as Carlos Montenegro, Augusto Céspedes, and Víctor Paz Estenssoro. To the left of the MNR, the pro-Moscow PIR also had significant connections in mining districts, such as Siglo XX.

The other key force was the POR, which would emerge in this period as one of the most influential Trotskyist parties in the world. In 1946, the federation's fourth congress issued a radical program—the Thesis of Pulacayo—that bore the stamp of Guillermo Lora, a tireless, prolific ideologue of Bolivian Trotskyism. According to the Pulacayo document, due to the backward stage of capitalist development in Bolivia, there was no national bourgeoisie capable of carrying out the necessary transformation of social and economic conditions. It was thus incumbent upon the Bolivian proletariat to assume the role of vanguard leadership in order to bring about the permanent revolution.

Workers faced two historic challenges, according to the Thesis. One was the task of democratic revolution, unifying the nation by attacking feudal institutions such as the hacienda as well as breaking the imperialist stranglehold of the United States. Second was the task of socialist revolution, attacking the internal capitalist regime that organized Bolivian mining and industry so as to forge proletarian control over the state and economic production. To advance this agenda, the Thesis called for direct worker intervention (*co-gobierno*) in the management of the mines, as well as worker militias trained to fight in a potential civil war. The document's simultaneous emphasis on wage demands, however, reflected a tension between "economism" and proletarian political autonomy that would mark the mine workers' movement over subsequent decades.

The Thesis of Pulacayo proclaimed the tactical necessity of a united front in which proletarians would receive the backing of the peasantry, artisans, and petty bourgeoisie. Yet the key to the political ascendancy of the miners turned out be their alliance—mediated by Juan Lechín, the magnetic executive secretary of the mine workers' federation—with the MNR. From the revolutionary left, the POR saw the alliance as providing potential access to the state as well as necessary middle-class support should strike actions lead to a military confrontation with the government.

For the MNR, facing increasing hostility from the political elite and the military, the alliance offered an alternative base of support, one that could be mobilized to overthrow the *rosca*. In the six-year period (known as the *sexenio*) from 1946–52, the MNR would carry out a dozen coup attempts. The strategy ultimately proved effective in bringing the MNR to power, yet the party was also transformed by its relationship with the mine workers. By the late 1940s, as a revolutionary conjuncture took shape, the MNR was increasingly pushed to the left, declaring its support for strikes in the cities and mining centers and taking up radical positions advocated by the POR in favor of the working class.

In August and September of 1949, the MNR led a revolt that served as a rehearsal for the insurrection of 1952. While the military succeeded in repressing the movement, rebels temporarily took over the regions of Cochabamba, Sucre, and Potosí, and established a provisional government in Santa Cruz, which was still a frontier city of 50,000 people. The conflict also revealed a deepening polarization between the civilian forces of the middle-class MNR and mine workers, on the one hand, and the oligarchy defended by the armed forces, on the other. When the MNR triumphed with an outright majority in the 1951 presidential elections, only to have the results annulled by an anti-communist military junta, conditions were ripe for a revolutionary solution. On 9 April 1952, the MNR finally made its move. It initially counted on the loyalty of the police force, but the military's concerted stand forced the MNR to distribute arms to workers and civilians, a measure it had not taken in 1949. After armed miners marched on La Paz and engaged in brief but intense urban clashes that left 600 dead, the military ranks finally collapsed and the army surrendered on 11 April to the son of Hernando Siles, Hernán Siles Zuazo.[5]

Sea Change

As in Mexico, the uprising in Bolivia amounted to a major social revolution with a powerful nationalist though not socialist thrust. Both revolutions were led by urban middle-class reformists confronting oligarchic elites, and both depended for their initial success on shifting tactical, though not yet clientelist, alliances with insurgent workers and peasants.[6] It was the powerful mobilization of these subaltern groups that swept away the remnants of the old order: landlords in the countryside, the *rosca* elite and its retinue in the mining centers and the capital, as well as the repressive apparatus of the state. The MNR's revolutionary measures—first and foremost, the fulfillment of the old radical vision of "mines to the state and land to the people"—were a response to active pressures from below that had accumulated since the era of the Chaco War.

Because of that very process of historical accumulation since the 1930s, the revolution possessed a deep national-popular dimension. The convergent struggles of indigenous peasants and proletarians, in combination with progressive middle-class elements, created a powerful political bloc. It opposed a seigneurial oligarchic regime that violently repressed the most vulnerable sectors of its own populace while willingly answering to international capitalism and the hemispheric interests of the United States. Popular forces aspired instead to a sovereign new national order that would protect the country's wealth of natural resources, foment domestic growth and social welfare, and allow more direct political participation in national affairs.

There were multiple tensions and contradictions within this bloc. Despite the rural origins of much of the mining labor force, relations between workers and peasants were marked by a sense of cultural and class distance. Urban workers' organizations held the upper hand politically, and tended to look upon their rural comrades as natural followers. Antonio Alvarez Mamani, an Indian peasant leader in the 1940s, would later remember with bitterness the disregard that Lechín and Lora displayed towards peasant leaders in political assemblies: "They invited me several times to their meetings in Oruro. I went and saw that mainly they smoked cigarettes and spoke about the orders of the party, while we, the peasants, were supposed to be there like spectators in the cinema or the theater, without voice or vote, just as listeners, so that afterwards we would go spread those orders in the countryside."[7]

The contrast between Mamani's statement and how Manuel Michel had described his relation with urban radicals in 1927 is stark. Where Mamani emphasized only hierarchy and distance, Michel, while noting hierarchy between "indigenous and gentlemen," had emphasized solidarity and shared humanity: "They have understood their duty to put themselves on the side of the indigenous race, and they do it disinterestedly, giving us good advice, indicating to us the authorities to whom we should direct our demands, taking an interest in our uplift." He insisted these were "people of justice; they are human." But by the 1940s, the balance of forces within the political opposition had tilted away from indigenous movements and demands.

In the end, however, the convergence of indigenous peasant and proletarian struggles proved politically potent, and the different insurgent groups benefited tangibly when revolutionary forces triumphed. The first major achievement was the nationalization of the tin mines. This gave the state direct control over the country's historically profitable mineral reserves, and it simultaneously handed union forces a key role in the management of resources. The miners were a self-appointed vanguard of maybe 6,000, claiming to represent a workforce that numbered 53,000, about 3 percent of the total population in 1952. Despite their light demographic weight, miners produced 95 percent of exports, and provided 45 percent of government revenues.[8]

Their strategic political role in the April revolution also meant that the Bolivian Workers Central (COB)—the trade union umbrella organization founded within a week of the victory and headed by mine workers' representative Juan Lechín—exercised an effective dual power alongside the MNR government. This was evident in the role of "worker-ministers" in the cabinet, at one point numbering five, who could directly advocate for the interests of labor. Even more strikingly, the Bolivian military was not rebuilt, and worker militias retained control over arms.

The agrarian reforms carried out via land takeovers, and ratified by the MNR as the Decree of Land Reform on August 2, 1953, were the second deepest in Latin America after Mexico's. Between the founding of the republic and the national revolution, and mainly after 1881, Indian communities diminished from 11,000 to some 3,799, while the number of landless families had risen to 216,000.[9] But in 1952–3, land takeovers spread throughout the countryside, picking up from the 1946–7 cycle of mobilization. Throughout the departments of La Paz, Oruro, and Cochabamba, in northern Potosí and parts of Chuquisaca, community peasants, tenants, and rural laborers destroyed hacienda buildings, seized estates, and redistributed land among themselves. Lacking government protection of their persons and properties, landlords and their families simply fled. The MNR was thus forced into revolutionary redistribution of land, a process it had not initially advocated, with Decree Law 3464, signed in front of 100,000 peasants in Ucureña, Cochabamba, where rural trade unionism had taken root after the Chaco War.[10] Especially in the western highlands and valleys, the 6 percent of landowners who owned 92 percent of cultivated land faded into political insignificance and the 60 percent who owned just 0.2 percent of the land assumed a new importance.

Indian peasants also benefited directly from the extension of the franchise, which eliminated literacy and occupational requirements and expanded the voting base from 200,000 to 1,000,000.[11] Furthermore, the MNR instituted an important education reform, responding to the demands that indigenous leaders had been making for decades. The government offered access to public education that would be free and available to the citizenry regardless of social class or ethnicity in all regions of the country. Taken together, land distribution, the creation of MNR peasant trade unions and rural schools, and voting rights gave the MNR something like hegemony over the indigenous peasant communities and individual smallholders.[12]

Nationalism prevailed ideologically in 1952, despite the importance of socialist elements within the mine workers' movement. As the official newspaper, *La Nación*, put it: "Our revolution is not social but national."[13] There were also *indigenista* features to official revolutionary culture—the great muralists Walter Solón Romero and Miguel Alandia Pantoja, for example, created powerful depictions of Indian suffering, resistance, and redemption. Yet these *indigenista* elements were subsumed within a progressive nationalist ideology centered on *mestizaje* or race mixture. *Mestizaje* implied a distillation of Bolivia's distinct Spanish and Indian racial and civilizational essences into a blended national unity.

The government preferred to drop ethnic distinctions for class identification—the country's rural denizens would be celebrated as industrious "peasant" laborers rather than stigmatized with the colonial label of "Indians." There were echoes here of Independence hero José de San Martín's call for unified national identity: "In future the aborigines shall not be called Indians or natives; they are children and citizens of Peru, and they shall be known as Peruvians."[14] In this case, class and ethnic cleavages would be reconciled in "Bolivian" national identity. The MNR thus tended to see cross-class alliance and unitary citizenship as the fulfillment of the earlier yet frustrated promise of independence in 1825. Revolutionary consciousness for creole nationalists and socialists alike did not call up the memory of 1781, with its associations of racial antagonism.[15] The national revolution brought deep transformation in political economic conditions—control over natural resources and land, state and class power—as well as in subjectivity—class, ethnic, and national identity—for those who participated. These changes would have lasting historical consequences in terms of political imagination. Not least, they would serve as a historical reference point for those sustaining revolutionary aspirations in the future.

Ebb Tide

The MNR regime shifted in an increasingly conservative direction over the course of the 1950s. President Víctor Paz Estenssoro (first three terms, 1952–6, 1960–4, August–November 1964) was seen in Washington as a liberal modernizer, not a radical. Hence, rather than mount reactionary coups to reverse the revolutionary process (as in Guatemala or Iran), under President Eisenhower the US government sought to re-channel the revolution into a new client-state relationship. Paz's independent foreign policy in 1952–3, based on anti-Americanism, lasted only as long as Bolivia's nationalized mines were without an American tin contract. Minerals accounted for 95 percent of Bolivian exports in 1950. By the end of 1952, with inflation rising and foreign exchange nearly used up, 70 percent of mining exports had been suspended due to nationalization. As President Paz had said in Congress, best to avoid the fate of Iran; there, efforts to nationalize the petroleum industry led the US government to overthrow a democratically elected government and install a right-wing dictator. After June 1953, under the first Eisenhower administration, the Paz administration depended on US tin contracts and its economic, food, and development aid—all contingent on a commitment to anti-communist counterinsurgency.

Lechín at first pulled organized labor, even the radicalized workers in the miners' trade union federation (FSTMB), in an economistic, reformist direction, firmly within the orbit of Paz and the MNR, and loosely aligned with the US government and Cold War labor. His personal sway was crucial, since many miners belonged to the Trotskyist Revolutionary Workers Party (POR) or the Bolivian Communist Party (PCB), and nearly all were anti-imperialist. But the decline in the revolutionary alliance accelerated in the aftermath of 1956. In exchange for foreign aid, the IMF called for—and the US government coordinated—an economic "stabilization" plan that curtailed wage increases for workers as well as state expenditures, subsidies, and tariffs. At the same time, the US instigated the reconstruction of Armed Forces that could subdue the potential threat of internal unrest.

In 1957, the FSTMB demanded a salary hike and broke with the politics of "co-government." The left wing of the COB split over whether to strike. The MNR—which started out as a hierarchical, paramilitary organization with a cellular structure—splintered under Hernán Siles Zuazo, leader of the 1952 insurrection.[16] The middle class fled toward to the MNR's right wing, to the military itself, or to the *falangistas*, the Bolivian Socialist Phalange (FSB), which had a regional base in the east in Santa Cruz, where a political culture of revanchist *caudillismo* prevailed. This situation of fragmentation began under Siles (1956–60), and intensified during Paz Estenssoro's second administration (1960–4).

Paz Estenssoro continued to bid for modernizing development that was hitched to the US and the Cold War in the hemisphere. Under the Alliance for Progress (1961–3), the US promoted structural economic advances that were to overcome poverty and social polarization, and thereby counter the spreading influence of the Cuban revolution. With Cuba in the back of his mind, it was no wonder Kennedy praised compliant Bolivia: "This great revolution has blazed a path for others to follow."[17] Meanwhile, under US tutelage, the Bolivian military moved increasingly from Hemispheric Defense to National Security. Rather than a prosperous civil democracy, what emerged in this period was growing conflict and polarization that led to the imposition of a military dictatorship in November 1964, with US Army Colonel and CIA Chief Edward Fox acting as "the guiding hand."[18] Hopes of advancing the revolution would be shelved, though not for long.

7

Dictatorship, Democracy, and the National State, 1964–84

In August of 1964, Víctor Paz Estenssoro had been elected to a third term. Three months later, he was out of office, the victim of a military coup. Mounting internal opposition to Paz came from Lechín and the trade union movement, from Hernán Siles and the left wing of the MNR, and from the right-wing Patriotic Reason (RADEPA) party. From without, the US sought a stable partner who could keep the threat of popular power and revolutionary contagion from Cuba at bay. The reconstructed military assumed the task of imposing order, and General René Barrientos Ortuño emerged as the man for the job. The shift to the right—that Paz himself had initiated before 1956, steered in the early 1960s, and that now brought about his own ouster—was finally sealed.

Central to counter-revolution was the task of driving a wedge between workers and peasants. After retaking the miners' share of state power in the 1950s, Paz had increased rural land redistribution between 1960 and 1964 to this effect. The Barrientos regime then worked assiduously to strengthen the conservative alliance between peasants and the post-revolutionary state that would last into the Banzer period of the 1970s. But just as the support of the peasantry was a pre-requisite for the rise of dictatorships, so the loss of that support would lead to their undoing. Under new conditions in the 1970s, the balance of repression—focused almost exclusively on miners and the COB in the 1950s and '60s—shifted to include the countryside, and the dictatorial state confronted autonomous peasant organizing and direct action.

The military dictatorships, increasingly tied to lowland agribusiness and the cocaine trade, polarized politics such that a new national-popular bloc came to cohere around the COB; more and more, the dictatorial state faced off against society itself. The peasantry played a key role in this struggle, especially as a new generation of highland trade union leaders grew up and adopted an increasingly assertive indigenous identity. When the communities broke away from the state pact in the 1970s and realigned with the COB, national-popular forces would finally be able to beat back reactionary military forces and usher in a return to democracy.

The Military-Peasant Pact

In the 1960s, state rule continued to rest solidly on the support of the peasantry, even after the MNR was displaced by the new authoritarian regime. Though the US government might have preferred an institutional manager like General Alfredo Ovando Candia, it needed a *caudillo* like Barrientos to control the peasantry. Barrientos was a reactionary demagogue who spoke fluent Quechua, which he used to build a constituency in his native Cochabamba countryside. His solid anti-communist credentials included having sent peasant militias from Cochabamba to fight insurgent miners' and left parties as early as 1959.

Barrientos's alliance—reinforced through official visits to remote villages and hamlets in a helicopter donated by Gulf Oil, from which Barrientos distributed soccer balls, television sets, and bicycles—came to be known as the "military-peasant pact," and formed the bulwark of US-supported counter-revolution in the cities and mining enclaves. The San Juan massacre of June 1967 was the most notorious case of post-revolutionary state violence. On a night of revelry marking the winter festival of San Juan, the army surrounded and captured the mining camps of Siglo XX and Llallagua under cover of darkness, and then opened fire leaving 87 men, women, and children dead in northern Potosí. Though miners struck for the next two weeks in protest, they had suffered a historic defeat. Their "peasant brothers"—Quechua-Aymaras and mestizos—were against them, or at best indifferent. This is what René Zavaleta referred to as the "isolation" of the Bolivian proletariat.[1]

This split between urban, proletarian left forces and the rural peasantry was essential to a counter-revolutionary project against which Che Guevara and his comrades of the National Liberation Army (ELN) did not stand a chance—the *foco* was dismantled in a matter of months in 1967. In contrast to trade union struggle, guerrilla armies lacked historical roots in Bolivian soil, other than small-scale defensive campaigns fought in the 1780s and 1810s.[2] Nonetheless, through myth and memory, the ELN would inspire revolutionary student youth through the 1980s, and Che Guevara would acquire the status of popular Andean saint.

In 1969, after Barrientos's death in a helicopter crash, a new national-revolutionary turn took place. This was most immediately modeled on General Juan Velasco Alvarado's military government in Peru, but also reminiscent of the Toro and Busch regimes in the late 1930s. A brilliant campaign waged by socialist writer, orator, and senator, Marcelo Quiroga Santa Cruz, led to Bolivia's second major nationalization of strategic natural resources. The government, now in the hands of Gen. Alfredo Ovando Candia, confiscated the holdings of Gulf Oil in October 1969. There followed the rise of a leftist general, Juan José Torres, to power in October 1970—less than a month before Salvador Allende entered office in Chile—and the formation of the Popular Assembly (AP) in June 1971.

The AP was a radical parliament of sorts, an alphabet soup of left groups and trade unions, in which peasants—principally lowland colo-nizers from the Maoist Independent Bloc—had few delegates.[3] The reason given for near-complete exclusion of Aymara-Quechua peasant represen-tatives from the highlands and valleys was that they would have tilted the Assembly toward the conservative military establishment. In terms of political consequences, however, their exclusion proved to be costly to the left and the working class and peasantry.

Meanwhile, entrepreneurs from Santa Cruz, connected to the private sector in petroleum, coffee, and sugar—all in danger of being nationalized to extinc-tion—waged a successful campaign of economic sabotage against the AP similar to those that would soon plague Allende's Chile. They found their political proxy in *cruceño* (from Santa Cruz) General Hugo Banzer Suárez, an uncharismatic career military man who was trained and trusted by the US.[4] Backed by the Brazilian military, and supported domestically by the Civic Committee of Santa Cruz, the FSB, and right-wing factions of the MNR, Banzer began to organize and agitate against the "communist danger."

In August 1971, the Popular Assembly easily gave way to reaction in the form of the *banzerato* (1971–8), a military dictatorship dedicated to reversing the direction of Ovando-Torres's radical nationalist drift. Following Banzer's bumbling coup, in which 98 people were killed and 506 injured in the first thirty hours, oppositional politics would be conducted in exile and clandestinity. Public policy, on the other hand, became the preserve of the military and their closest advisors, especially after economic reforms compelled by the IMF triggered popular unrest in the early 1970s. The *banzerato* prefigured the overthrow of Allende and the implementation of neoliberalism under General Pinochet in 1973, but also led to the end of the "military-peasant pact," which had been the principal domestic support for the US-supported and -funded counterinsurgency.

Indian Peasant Autonomy

With the left and organized labor on the defensive, Banzer took less interest in the state's traditional rural base. Rather than hand out parcels of land to small peasants in the highlands and valleys, the *cruceño* dictator favored large concessions to estate owners in the eastern lowlands. When the government followed IMF directives to devalue the currency in 1972 and then removed subsidies on basic goods and subsidies in early 1974, it provoked hardship in the countryside. Yet Banzer had no compunction about calling in troops to put down protest, and the Massacre of the Valley took place in Cochabamba, the very region where Barrientos had staked his authority. The death knell in January 1974 was not only for between 80 and 200 peasant protesters in Tolata, but for the military-peasant pact itself.

The breakdown of revolutionary state hegemony and of the durability of the authoritarian and counter-insurgent regimes was also due to the rise of a new generation of young peasant leaders without older ties of loyalty to the MNR and the military. Genaro Flores—who was elected Secretary General in the Fourth Congress of the National Peasant Workers' Confederation (CNTC) two weeks before Banzer's coup in 1971—openly repudiated MNR paternalism and what he called political "*pongueaje*" (servility). Though much less visible than left party and proletarian militants in the Popular Assembly, the Aymara trade-unionists in La Paz, Oruro, and Potosí renewed Indian peasant traditions of struggle and left their stamp on contemporary political culture.

The two critical political currents of *indianismo* and *katarismo* developed rapidly, first with Torres in power, then against the Banzer dictatorship. Both were indebted to the same discursive source, Fausto Reinaga, a fiery and prolific ideologue who had passed through affiliations with the MNR and Marxism before establishing his own (largely discursive) Party of Aymara and Kechua Indians (later Indian Party) in 1962. Reinaga criticized the use of "*mestizaje*" as a national revolutionary ideology and placed colonialism and "the Indian question" at the heart of his radical reinterpretation of Bolivia's past, present, and future.[5]

In 1973, *kataristas*—reclaiming the legacy of Tupaj Katari, his consort Bartolina Sisa, and Zárate Villca—issued the landmark "Manifesto of Tiwanaku." The document noted the gains of the national revolution as well as its limits—among other points, Aymara-Quechua peasants were "foreigners" in their own country due to the culturally homogenizing policies of the MNR and the military. In this vision, peasant class consciousness and Aymara and Quechua ethnic consciousness were complementary rather than contradictory. Also, since they saw capitalism as well as colonialism at the root of contemporary exploitation, *kataristas* showed a willingness to seek out potential class allies.

> The miners, factory workers, builders, transport workers, and the impoverished middle classes are all our brothers and sisters, victims in different ways of the same exploitation, descendants of the same race and united in solidarity for the same ideals of struggle and liberation. Only united can we achieve a great future for our country.[6]

Indianistas, on the other hand, had less of a base in the peasant trade union movement and their political discourse placed greater emphasis on racial than class domination. Hewing closely to Reinaga, and organizing themselves in small party factions, they spurned alliances with what they branded the "mestizo-creole" left, arguing that it reproduced elements of racist paternalism characteristic of the national revolutionary governments and military dictatorships.[7]

In the meantime, however, the *banzerato* had transformed the political-economic geography of Bolivia. Relying politically on the support of right-wing agro-industrial entrepreneurs who dealt in soy beans, rice, and above all, cotton in lowland Santa Cruz, Banzer generously subsidized the cotton growers' association, ADEPA, using government revenues from soft loans from the World Bank and taxes on the state petroleum company, YFPB. When crisis hit the cotton industry in 1975–6, a group of *cruceño* landlord-entrepreneurs like Guillermo "Willy" Banzer Ojopi, Roberto Suárez Gómez, later known as "the king of cocaine," and José Roberto Gasser—whose family financed Banzer's coup in 1971—diversified into narcotics production and sale, laundering money in the Banco Agrícola. Through the Condor Plan, a regional counterinsurgency network established in coordination with the US Southern Command based in Panamá, cocaine production in Bolivia became tied to counter-revolutionary politics.[8] In the Southern Cone, the criminal, mafia-like dictatorships installed in Chile and Uruguay in 1973 reinforced Banzer's right turn after 1974.[9]

This reactionary and regional bloc of support was not, however, broad enough to sustain the Banzer regime. Internationally it was hamstrung by its unconstitutional status and human rights violations. Domestically, it could not keep inflation under control, count on strong middle-class backing, or contain proliferating popular resistance. In spite of divisions within the opposition, hunger strikes led by wives of detained mining leaders demanding a general amnesty, backed by diplomatic pressure from the early Carter administration, brought down the Banzer regime with suprising ease between the end of 1977 and July 1978.[10]

By the late 1970s, *kataristas* found deep support for their project among the Quecha-Aymara peasant base, and the era of MNR-military hegemony, at least in rural trade unions where much of community politics was now conducted, was over.[11] The key role of unionized peasant communities in the road blockades and general strike that reversed the coup of Col. Alberto Natusch Busch in November 1979 revealed that the balance of opposition forces had also changed fundamentally.[12]

Founded in June 1979, the new Trade Union Confederation of Bolivian Peasant Workers (CSUTCB) and its *katarista* leader, Genaro Flores, had become essential to popular organization and resistance, even if proletarian centrality remained a fact and, to some, a matter of faith. Orthodox assumptions that proletarians constituted the necessary vanguard for future democratic and socialist revolution continued to prevail within the Trade Union Federation of Bolivian Mine Workers (FSTMB), the COB, and the left, which was now led by Movement of the Revolutionary Left (MIR) and Socialist Party-1 (PS1), rather than the Bolivian Communist Party (PCB) and the Revolutionary Workers' Party (POR). Similar to the Chayanta rebellion of 1927 or the agrarian unrest of 1946–7, 1979 was a high point of community mobilization that left lasting effects, even if the national-popular convergence of workers and the left with Aymara and Quechua peasants would be a temporary rather than permanent feature of the new political landscape.[13]

Regime Change

The landed, narco-paramilitary right based in the eastern lowlands of Santa Cruz and Beni looked on with alarm at the fall of Banzer in 1978 and the defeat of Natusch Busch in 1979. They were also disturbed by the political rise of the Democratic Popular Unity (UDP), a center-left coalition backed by the COB and led by Jaime Paz Zamora's MIR, Marcelo Quiroga Santa Cruz's PS1, the PCB, and Siles Zuazo's Revolutionary Nationalist Movement of the Left (MNRI). Any UDP government, they feared, would collaborate with the US Drug Enforcement Agency to eliminate its political rivals on the right. They therefore backed General Luis García Meza's "cocaine coup" on 17 July 1980, by which time roughly 70 percent of cocaine in the US had its origins in Bolivian coca paste (processed into cocaine in Colombia).

García Meza also enjoyed the external support of the Brazilian and Argentine military governments and hosted a cast of shadowy fascist figures, including Nazis new and old like Klaus Barbie, "the butcher of Lyon," Albert Van Ingelgom, a chief functionary of Auschwitz, and Joachim Fiebelkorn. With Interior Minister Col. Luis Arce Gómez overseeing the dirty work, the coup was followed by a brief but intense phase of repression. In little more than a year, approximately 1,000 people labeled "subversives" were killed or disappeared. Prominent among them was the charismatic Socialist Party leader Marcelo Quiroga Santa Cruz, who was singled out for assassination in the original paramilitary attack on the headquarters of the COB in downtown La Paz. *Katarista* leader Genaro Flores suffered a crippling gunshot wound, but managed to escape from the building with his life.

The ties between the corrupt military brass and lowland drug traffickers were exemplified by the fact that Roberto Suárez Gómez, a leader in the Santa Cruz-Beni cocaine circuit, was the cousin of Arce Gómez. With Arce Gómez coordinating taxation of the lucrative cocaine trade, García Meza and his cronies quickly accumulated extravagant wealth and property.

One US State Department official commented: "For the first time the mafia has bought itself a government."[14]

International repudiation and domestic resentment, including among marginalized sectors of the armed forces, obliged the narco-military dictator García Meza to step down in August 1981. A de facto military junta under Gen. Celso Torrelio Villa and then Gen. Guido Vildoso Calderón persisted under *garciamecista* influence until COB-led mass mobilizations finally forced the regime to relinquish power in October 1982. In a congressional vote, Hernán Siles Zuazo—the historic leader of the April Revolution in 1952—was elected president, and Jaime Paz Zamora vice-president, on the Democratic Popular Unity (UDP) ticket.

The center-left UDP took charge amidst high expectations and a robust sense of popular power. The national-popular alliance—the COB along with the emergent and autonomous CSUTCB, left political parties, and progressive fractions of the middle class—had managed to overthrow three military dictatorships (Banzer in 1977, Natusch in 1979, García Meza and his successors by 1982) in quick succession, and bring representative democracy into being through mass collective action. This democratic opening was a major stride forward, allowing many on the left to anticipate deeper revolutionary change in the imaginable future.

The UDP's own steps, however, failed to measure up to expectations. When the FSTMB and the left continued to pressure the government with strikes, the coalition fractured and Siles Zuazo was quickly isolated, lacking a constituency except for the fraction of the MNR that he led. As soon as he accepted strike demands and began to negotiate, other sectors followed the example set by the FSTMB, and strike activity rose throughout the UDP period from 1982–5. For their part, opposed to mass mobilization in the western highlands and valleys, regional elites in the eastern lowlands of Santa Cruz and Beni—the bastion of the dictatorships—organized strikes through their civic committees.

The UDP government emitted ever more currency to cover the cost of the agreements it signed with unions and civic committees, and in the early 1980s Bolivia became the country with the highest inflation rate in the world. The middle class watched its savings and income disappear, which opened the way for their initial embrace of a neoliberal solution to the crisis. In its view, the left had proven unable to govern, and was held responsible for economic crisis. For the left itself, initial hopes of a transition from "dictatorship" to "democracy" to "socialism," which had brought the UDP into being, were shattered against the rocks of mismanagement and crisis. The political momentum accumulated through the national-popular mobilizations of the late 1970s and early 1980s was squandered, and the revolutionary horizon dimmed.

PART III

The Present as History, 1985–2006

Coca Growers Marching, October 2004. © Noah Friedman-Rudovsky

8

Neoliberal Ascendance and the "War on Drugs," 1985–99

The New Political Economy

With inflation running as high as 20,000 percent in 1984–5—one of the highest rates in world history—President Siles Zuazo called early elections, and Paz Estenssoro took his third and final turn in office.[1] In a dramatic reversal of the 1952 national revolution, Paz Estenssoro now set out to dismantle the dependent state capitalism he had helped erect during his first term. He called on a young, American-educated technocrat—Gonzalo Sánchez de Lozada—to redesign the relationship between the state, society, and the economy, which resulted in a neoliberal blueprint: Supreme Decree 21060. Following the advice of Harvard economist Jeffrey Sachs, whose neoliberal "shock treatments" would later be applied to Eastern Europe and the former Soviet Union to devastating effect, the New Economic Policy (NPE) cut government spending, overhauled the monetary system—thereby bringing a halt to hyperinflation while plunging the country into recession—and encouraged foreign investment.

The state tin mines, which provided the bulk of Bolivian government revenue before and after 1952, were privatized as the price of tin collapsed on the international market, and more than 20,000 miners were "relocated" (a euphemism for firing and displacement) from the western highlands in Oruro and Potosí. Those who "relocated" to the cities were joined by other peasant migrants escaping from the deteriorating conditions in the countryside. Their influx could not be absorbed given the decline in domestic manufacturing and employment, and the precariousness of urban labor intensified. By 1991, at least 45,000 jobs had been lost in mining and state administration, and another 35,000 through factory shut-downs. Close to 60 percent of the urban labor force fended for itself through "informal" activities, and of those families, half were unable to meet basic food costs.[2]

Those miners and peasants who descended to the eastern lowland frontier to grow coca helped supply the internal (mainly indigenous) demand for coca leaf as well as the rising cocaine economy.[3] In the 1980s, coca paste and cocaine became the nation's most profitable export commodities, their value approaching or exceeding that of total legal exports. The income and jobs linked to coca and cocaine cushioned the economy's fall after neoliberalism's crippling blows to production.[4]

Arguably Latin America's most combative proletariat in the second half of the twentieth century, the tin miners were broken when Paz Estenssoro—who had first risen to power on the strength of the miners' militias in 1952—crushed their "March in Defense of Life" in 1986. The FSTMB and the COB would never again demonstrate the same capacity to agglutinate a broad array of forces around a national-popular program. Left political parties, which had long followed in the wake of, rather than led, national-popular movements, declined precipitously after 1986.

Some of their middle-class cadre made an exodus into the more lucrative world of NGOs, and many withdrew from political action with a sense of disillusion and defeat. Some of the intelligentsia, whose role from the 1930s through the 1980s was often militant or expressed principled dissent, either guarded silence or actively collaborated with the new regime in the name of strengthening and amplifying "democracy," ensuring "governability," improving "competitivity," recognizing "multi-ethnic, pluricultural" diversity, and so on. The exhaustion and trauma of the UDP period thus led to political demobilization, a widely felt desire for stability, and an unobstructed opening for neoliberal initiatives.

Once neoliberal restructuring had begun, the CSUTCB launched a struggle with proletarian organizations over representation and leadership within the COB. The traditional urban trade union leadership, clinging to classic assumptions about industrial workers' vanguard role in revolutionary transitions, refused to transform itself, thereby sealing its own demise. Peasant political organization was thus forced in new, more autonomous directions in the late 1980s and 1990s, and class struggle was increasingly recast as, or supplanted by, ethnic struggle. As

Aymara nationalism grew stronger, more radical *indianista* tendencies superseded *katarismo* in an overall climate of factionalism within the CSUTCB.

The Tupac Katari Guerrilla Army (EGTK)—which came to have over four hundred cells on the high plains, and was made up almost exclusively of Aymara peasant cadre—made its appearance after 1986. However, lacking allies or political legitimacy, it posed no general threat to the neoliberal regime, and was easily wiped out in the early 1990s.[5] Other ethnic organizations outside and critical of the CSUTCB, often with the backing of NGOs and foreign donors, pursued the reconstitution of territorial federations of *ayllus* and traditional indigenous authority systems in Oruro, La Paz, and Potosí. While few took such efforts seriously at the time, the influence of Indian intellectuals and indigenous activism continued to spread. In 1990, newly organized groups from the tropical lowlands mobilized in the historic "March for Territory and Dignity," which called attention to the incursions of lumber firms and cattle ranchers and obtained presidential recognition of seven indigenous territories.

Coca and *Cocaleros*

In the late 1980s to early 1990s, with the COB and the CSUTCB in factionalist decline, the coca growers' movement, 60,000-strong and led by a young Evo Morales, offered the only vibrant national-popular resistance to US imperialism in Bolivia. In 1988, the US-imposed Law 1008 criminalized coca production outside restricted areas and beyond limited yields, and set the bases for forced eradication. Enforcement efforts continued to target peasant growers and petty traffickers as opposed to cocaine lords, and President George H. W. Bush's "war on drugs" in the Andes compelled increasing militarization of interdiction efforts. The coca growers' movement—organized through local and regional trade union federations, as well as rudimentary self-defense militias—responded with impressive determination and mobilization, denying any responsibility for drug-trafficking and exalting the coca leaf as part of millennial Andean cultural tradition. President Jaime Paz Zamora (1989–93) angered the US government with his campaign of "coca diplomacy," which drew upon producers' own emphasis on the distinction between coca and cocaine. Their collective political strength grew in the early 1990s, and when Gonzalo Sánchez de Lozada and the MNR took over in 1993, they had become a movement to contend with.

It is crucial to remember that in the late 1980s and 1990s, first Paz Zamora, then Sánchez de Lozada (1993–7) forged tacit pacts with the coca growers: while telling the US Embassy they planned to comply with Law 1008, in practice they refused to implement forced eradication. This gave the neoliberal coalitions room to deepen their policies without having to confront the coca growers directly, thereby deflecting anti-imperialism toward the US Embassy, which directed operations using units it had trained and equipped. The program of privatization and shrinking state "development" initiatives, of course, created the conditions whereby *only* coca farming could provide a livelihood for tens of thousands of families, a population of some 200,000 people whose limited contact with the state occurred mainly when military-police "joint task forces" made occasional incursions.[6] "Alternative development" measures in coca-growing areas, highly touted by the US but scantily funded, have proven an almost complete failure. Through the 1990s, then, coca production and the laundering of cocaine money continued to help offset the worst effects of the neoliberal regime for the economy as a whole, and tempered hostility toward the governing parties.

For many, the "Patriotic Accord" government—a MIR-ADN coalition led by Jaime Paz Zamora which entered office in 1989—symbolized the cynical opportunism of the political class. Paz Zamora himself, like many of his former leftist "comrades" in the MIR, had endured political persecution during the *banzerato*. Yet as in the rest of Latin America, in the name of "democracy," the center-left cut the bureaucratic cake of clientelism and patronage with a party that had supported dictatorship (in the Bolivian case, Banzer's own ADN). Both MIR and ADN had become notorious for corruption and close ties to narco-traffickers. The US Embassy exposed and used these ties to pressure the Paz Zamora administration to continue the neoliberal reforms initiated under Paz Estenssoro.[7] Widespread disillusion with merely formal "democracy" was evident in the rise of so-called neo-populist parties appealing to marginalized urban sectors that cropped up during Paz Zamora's term. Conscience of the Fatherland (CONDEPA) and the Union of Civic Solidarity (UCS) were led by the popular media personality Carlos Palenque and the beer magnate Max Fernández respectively, entrepreneurial figures from outside the creole political caste.

The Poverty of Progress

After shedding his image as a North American-style technocrat, Sánchez de Lozada of the MNR took office in 1993 with a coherent hegemonic project: to deepen the neoliberal regime while stabilizing and legitimating it through innovative social reform. This was reflected in the surprising electoral alliance with *katarista* Vice-President Víctor Hugo Cárdenas, who was born and raised in an Aymara community on Lake Titicaca. *Katarismo* had already lost its trade union base and deteriorated into a cluster of fractious parties with minimal electoral presence, yet it retained an intellectual prestige represented most notably by Cárdenas. Though his MRTKL (Tupac Katari Revolutionary Movement of Liberation) party was tiny, Cárdenas was a respected public figure and university professor. The alliance helped Sánchez de Lozada project a multicultural agenda that would "include the excluded"—neoliberalism with a human, even Aymara, face. Overlooking his own party's functionaries, he effectively channeled formerly independent and progressive intellectual and professional energies toward a "modernized" state administration. A centerpiece of his program was the municipal decentralization of resources—known as Popular Participation—which provided state recognition for local communities, while attempting to marginalize their trade union representation. Cárdenas, a specialist in pedagogy, oversaw the multicultural Educational Reform, which sought to undermine the role of unionized schoolteachers.[8]

These reformist experiments gave a participatory democratic profile to a government fundamentally set on liquidating remaining state enterprises and opening up the country to foreign capital. Between 1995 and 1997, the national oil and gas, telecommunications, airline, electricity, and railroad companies were sold off. The privatization program—euphemistically called "Capitalization"—earned praise since the country would retain 50 percent ownership in the firms delivered into the hands of transnationals, and since profits would be put aside into retirement funds for the citizenry. Because of the thoroughness of the privatization and the successful marketing of the "reforms," the IMF and the World Bank held Bolivia up as a model for "Less Developed Countries" around the world.[9]

In spite of Sánchez de Lozada's internationally trumpeted "success" and the continuation of the modest economic growth that began under Paz Zamora, the limited nature of the gains obtained through reforms was becoming apparent to all by 1997. Privatization did attract foreign capital, as intended, but did not bring the touted benefits of economic reactivation and employment.[10] Popular Participation, spurring municipal conflicts over newly disbursed state funds while doing little to redress local economic stagnation, failed to garner grassroots support. Vice-President Cárdenas witnessed the frustration of educational reforms, and his unhappy marriage with Sánchez de Lozada confirmed *katarismo*'s decline as a movement and the skeptics' warnings about creole manipulation of Indian allies for purposes of symbolic politics. A shift away from neoliberal "populism" was also evident in the growing power of the authoritarian Minister of the President, Carlos Sánchez Berzaín, known by his nickname "The Fox."

After running for presidential office five times since 1982, Banzer finally returned to power as head of his party, ADN, in 1997. This marked a new low in the "democratic" period, with dark memories of dictatorship, a wellspring of corruption, and deepening disillusion with the political party establishment and the failed promises of Sánchez de Lozada's reforms—the continuity of which Banzer had been elected to guarantee.[11] The former dictator turned "democrat" had no agenda of his own, other than *Plan Dignidad*, which was the US Embassy's plan, not Banzer's: the forced eradication of coca, first in the Chapare, then in the Yungas. Even as coca production skyrocketed in Colombia under guerrilla and paramilitary supervision, the "zero coca" offensive in the Chapare was touted as an imperial success story.

Banzer, dying of cancer, turned his office over to Vice-President Jorge "Tuto" Quiroga in 2001, and by the time "Tuto" left office in 2002, 70 percent of all coca crops had allegedly been eradicated. Peasant families lost a way of life that had allowed them to survive the long-term crisis that neoliberalism had exacerbated. Despite resistance, coca growers could not stop the juggernaut of eradication on their own. While dozens died under Banzer between 1997 and 2001, more than thirty died in the "drug war" under "Tuto" in 2001–2 alone. As neoliberal democracy deteriorated, state violence increasingly called to mind the dictatorships "democracy" was supposed to replace.

9

The New Revolutionary Cycle, 2000–3

Economic Contractions

By the late 1990s, it was not only coca growers whose economic fortunes were in decline but, as in much of Latin America, that of the economy as a whole. Between 1997 and 2002, an estimated $600–$900 million in revenue and more than 50,000 jobs were lost annually as a result of eradication. The economic crisis that swept the region following the Asian financial crisis of 1997—which, as far as G-7 countries were concerned, had been contained in Brazil—meant that international financial flows dried up, and what had been a torrent of cash remittances from Bolivian migrant workers in Argentina dwindled to a trickle by the late 1990s.

The effects of privatization further darkened the economic panorama. Thousands of workers were laid off, pension funds languished, while foreign firms had limited incentives to provide dividends or invest profits locally. Railroad and airline assets were stripped and sold. Rents were transferred out of telecommunications, a formerly profitable sector for the state. The hydrocarbon sector sustained the greatest losses of all. In keeping with Sánchez de Lozada's legislation in 1996, the state firm in control of oil and gas, YPFB, was broken up and auctioned off, and the royalties to be paid by multinational firms under new contracts were lowered from 50 percent to 18 percent. Coveted gas fields like San Antonio and San Alberto, which had been identified but not put into use, were reclassified as "new" and subject to the reduced rates.

The reclassification alone would amount to a loss of hundreds of millions, if not billions of dollars, in state revenue over the forty-year period stipulated by new contracts. Just prior to its "capitalization," YPFB had been about to sign a joint pipeline deal with Petrobras, funded with international loan money, which would have generated $50 million per year in additional revenues for the next 40 years. Instead, private firms, taking advantage of the same loans offered to YPFB, entered the fray and reaped the benefits. From 1985–96, the National Treasury had received an average of $350 million annually from YPFB. After 1997, the National Treasury would no longer recuperate earlier levels of petroleum-gas revenue, and in some years, it was seven times lower ($50 million) than what it had been before 1997.[1]

A Bolivian government report issued in December 2003 examined operations of 200 petroleum multinationals worldwide and found that in Bolivia, BP-Amoco and Repsol YPF benefited from the lowest production and exploration costs in the world. On the world market, the cost of producing the equivalent of a barrel of petroleum was $5.60 in 2003, but in Bolivia, it cost Repsol $1, and BP-Amoco, $0.97. The cost of finding and developing a barrel, meanwhile, averaged $8.58 worldwide and $5.66 in Latin America, but it was $0.40 for Repsol YPF in Bolivia. This was twenty times lower than the world average, and fourteen times lower than the Latin American average. Further, whereas worldwide 80 percent of efforts to find gas fields failed, in Bolivia half succeeded. Between 1998 and 2002, BP-Amoco paid an average of $5.2 million, while Repsol YPF paid an average of just $4.3 million in taxes. According to a graph constructed by Barrows Company, Bolivia's share of taxes and royalties was by far the lowest on the continent—only Peru came close.[2]

Privatization had the perverse effect of creating rising budget deficits ($430 million in 1997 alone) due to shortfalls in revenue. Bolivian governments were largely dependent on external aid for essentials like the payment of salaries to public employees, and Banzer's response to lower revenue was to cut spending and impose energy taxes that would be borne primarily by poor consumers. Sánchez de Lozada sought to continue this strategy, and the February 2003 tax riot in La Paz—against the IMF and the neoliberal political parties led by the MNR—would be one of the many unexpected results of privatization.

Opening Salvos

Working Bolivians were hit hard under Banzer, but they fought back. The "Water War" of April 2000 put Cochabamba on the map of anti-privatization struggles taking place around the world as the neoliberal order of the 1990s began to unravel following the "Battle for Seattle." In Bolivia, the stage for confrontation had been set in June 1997, when the World Bank told Sánchez de Lozada that if Cochabamba's water were to be privatized, the government would receive $600 million of debt relief. Then, in September 1999, the Banzer administration, led by Tuto Quiroga, leased Cochabamba's water supply until 2039 to the lone bidder: a transnational consortium called Aguas de Tunari, underwritten by Bechtel and Edison (Italy).

In December 1999, the "Coalition for the Defense of Water and Life" brought factory workers, farmers, coca growers, and green activists together to stop privatization. In January 2000, when massive rate hikes were announced, led by factory-worker Oscar Olivera, the *Coordinadora* organized a successful general strike in protest, shutting the city down, cutting it off from the rest of the country, and leading the multitude to take over the Plaza 14 de Septiembre in the city center. The Banzer administration agreed to review the new rates. "Market regulation" had meant that water constituted a quarter ($15) of household budgets for people earning minimum wage ($60 per month), and in some cases rates rose as much as 100 percent. With no change in sight, the *Coordinadora* called another strike for February, which the government declared illegal, sending in 1,200 soldiers and police to take control of the city. After more than 175 people were wounded, the government announced that rates would be lowered temporarily for six months.

As would happen in October 2003, there was a rapid radicalization of demands: after state violence escalated against unarmed demonstrators, the demand for the reduction of rates was superseded in favor of the outright rejection of multinational control over water and natural resources. The *Coordinadora* called for a "final battle" to begin in early April. The government's response was to make pre-emptive arrests of *Coordinadora* leaders and declare martial law on the fourth day of protests. The next day, Robinson Iriarte—a government sniper trained at the School of the Americas—dressed as a civilian, fired into a crowd of demonstrators, killing a seventeen-year-old. The city exploded in protest and barricades went up all over. By 4 April, the multitude had broken through the military cordon around the Plaza 14 de Septiembre, and an open-air assembly was held in which between 50,000 and 100,000 participated.

The next level of decision-making was the *Coordinadora*, in which delegates from smaller assemblies met in order to voice the concerns, perspectives, and demands of their sectors. In addition to workers, there were students and young people, environmentalists, intellectuals, irrigation farmers, neighborhood water committees. "Anyone could speak, but for you to be heard you had to take action," explains leader Oscar Olivera. "It was a time for talk, but not talk without action. The *Coordinadora* assemblies were where the communiqués and the strategic political analyses took place." Decisions taken were then discussed in open-air meetings or *cabildos* of 50,000–70,000 people—crowds too large to fit anywhere except public *plazas*. Here, final decisions were made: "At this level of assembly . . . there was an undercurrent of democratic participation and commentary." Although representatives addressed the crowd, the flow of discussion and proposal was not unidirectional. "The crowd responded to different proposals by expressing a collective sentiment, either by applauding or making disapproving noises such as boos or whistles. Sometimes leaders had to follow the people."[3] Aguas del Tunari was thrown out on 8 April, and the sale, distribution, and consumption of water was turned over to a collective, self-managed enterprise (SEMAPA). Furthermore, the call for a constitutional assembly was launched as a way to restructure the country and overcome the neoliberal crisis.[4]

The diversity of groups that participated in Cochabamba in April was impressive: *regantes* (small-scale coordinators of regional water distribution); valley and highland peasants (some indigenous); coca growers from the Chapare; the regional trade union federation, led by factory workers; students and progressive intellectuals; neighborhood associations, some of them led by re-localized miners; Aymara peasant migrants from the southern part of the city; street kids; the middle classes; and civic organizations. And insofar as the "Coalition for the Defense of Water and Life" was without hierarchical, *caudillo* leadership and uninfected by clientelism, it provided a dress rehearsal, at the municipal level, of the nationwide drama of October 2003, as well as an inspirational political model for metropolitan anti-globalization activists.[5]

President Banzer's setbacks did not stop in Cochabamba, however, for there were simultaneous mobilizations in the Yungas, northeast of La Paz, and the Lake Titicaca region, though there was no direct communication or coordination between them. From 5–9 April, the CSUTCB, under leadership of "El Mallku," Felipe Quispe, and the communities of the Aymara heartland of Omasuyos, established the most effective blockades since 1979.[6] Felipe Quispe had been a leading participant in Aymara *indianista* and guerrilla politics between the mid-1970s and 1990s. Like other Aymara leaders of his generation (excepting Víctor Hugo Cárdenas), he started out in rural trade union organizing. Following his release from prison in 1998, where he served a five-year sentence for his participation in the Tupac Katari Guerilla Army (EGTK), Quispe was elected Executive Secretary of the CSUTCB, and combined radical *indianista* discourse with militant peasant trade union organization, which had once been the domain of *kataristas*.

With the example of "El Mallku" and the communities of Omasuyos, Quechua-Aymara communities in Sucre, Oruro, and Potosí followed La Paz, as did coca growers in the Chapare. They were protesting proposed privatization of water at the national level as well as some aspects of the neoliberal land reform law (Ley INRA). In Achacachi, after two Aymaras were killed on 9 April, community members killed two army officials, and called on conscripts to join their community brothers and sisters in revolt. The insurgents looted the local Palace of Justice, the sub-Prefecture, the offices of Cotel (one of the private companies that stepped into the space left the by the much-reduced state telephone company), and then freed prisoners from the local jail. They proceeded to the hospital, where they killed an army captain whom they had earlier injured. Planes and 1,000 troops were mobilized against them, reconnoitering and strafing, searching and seizing. Yet communal power had temporarily supplanted state authority.

In the inter-Andean Yungas valleys, led by a young Dionisio Núñez, coca growers and peasant colonizers were protesting the threat of eradication that Banzer had announced in 1999. As a result of effective mobilization, the government was forced to sign an agreement to postpone forced eradication indefinitely. However limited regionally and sectorally, the mobilizations in Cochabamba, the Yungas, and the high plains were the most important popular shows of strength since the UDP was brought to power in 1982. And the concessions won were extracted from one of the most authoritarian political figures in contemporary Bolivia.

The carefully prepared road blockades of September–October 2000 on the high plains, and especially calls to march on the capital, raised the revolutionary specter of 1781 and the memory of Tupaj Katari, as food shortages in the capital multiplied over time. Insurgents refused to pay for water and land, or to cease growing and chewing coca. Quispe and his followers began to call for an Aymara nation composed of confederated communities. The idea of "two Bolivias," one indigenous, the other *q'ara* or non-Indian, not only circulated within rapidly radicalized Aymara circles, but also reverberated throughout society.[7]

Banzer had insurgent social movements in the highlands, highland valleys, and lowlands on his hands, and was at first helpless either to understand or combat them. What saved him was the failure of a strategic and tactical alliance between Quispe, Morales, and what remained of the *Coordinadora* in Cochabamba. Olivera was unable to mobilize significant numbers of foot soldiers for the September–October blockades, and Quispe and Morales sustained the *caudillo* rivalry that would plague the social movements until October 2003. Banzer negotiated with Quispe, thereby driving a wedge between him and representatives of the various other social movements. Quispe did, however, force the government to sign the "Isla del Sol Accords," according to which the government would address a long series of demands, including the repeal of Supreme Decree 21060, the neoliberal legislation of 1985.[8]

Harvesting Discontent

The first blows had been struck, and the triumphs for popular forces in the 2002 elections raised hopes of a gradual transition "from above" as a way out of the long-term crisis. Evo Morales achieved a near-victory in the presidential race, and the MAS, together with the Pachakuti Indigenous Movement (MIP), a radical Indianist party headed by Felipe Quispe, netted forty-two parliamentary seats between the two. The 2002 elections were a clear sign that the social movements—lowland and subtropical coca growers' trade union federations of the east and northeast, Quechua-Aymara communities in the highland valleys of Sucre and Potosí, Aymara communities of the western highlands of La Paz and Oruro, the civic, anti-privatization movement in the Cochabamba valley—had decisively altered the balance of formal political forces. A small but important sector of the urban middle class, fed up with neoliberal corruption, transnational domination, and economic crisis, also voted MAS. US Ambassador Manuel Rocha's threat to end aid to the country if it voted for Morales provoked nationalist ire, and gave MAS a further last-minute boost. No left party in Bolivia had ever achieved more than 5 percent of the national vote on its own, and Morales won 20.9 percent. Sánchez de Lozada, who obtained 22.5 percent of the vote, came to power with little public backing and no clear project. His governing coalition with MIR was weak and fragile.

From the time Sánchez de Lozada had helped institute the New

Economic Policy in 1985 to when he resumed the helm of the neoliberal state in the twenty-first century, per capita income had not risen; exports had grown by only 19 percent, while the population increased by 33 percent; the number of people working in the "informal sector" had risen from 58 percent to 68 percent. In 2002, the official unemployment rate had tripled over the previous thirteen years; the economy was in free fall for almost the fifth consecutive year; the balance of payments deficit accounted for $600 million annually. The percentage of those living in extreme poverty—as measured by the World Bank—grew from 36.4 percent in 1997 to 41.3 percent in 2002.

Measured by income and wealth, in 2003 Bolivia was one of the most unequal countries in the most inequitable region in the world—only Brazil was worse. The top 20 percent of the population owned 30 times more than the bottom 20 percent, and 60 percent lived in poverty (in rural areas, the figure was 90 percent). Infant mortality was 60 out of 1,000 births, and life expectancy was 63 years; in the Western Hemisphere, only Haiti posted more dismal numbers. The Bolivian "national economy" was composed of 550,000 peasant families combining market and subsistence activities, 770,000 informal urban "businesses," and no more than 500 capitalist enterprises.[9]

Misery was perhaps most concentrated in El Alto, a city in which women heads of households and their offspring dominated informal market activity. As a result of neoliberalism's effects on the countryside, El Alto received more migrants—two-thirds to three-quarters of them from the heavily Aymara provinces of La Paz—than any other Bolivian city. Population grew by roughly 9 percent annually, from about 300,000 in 1988 to 400,000 in 1992, to perhaps 800,000 by 2002. El Alto had the lowest urban level of basic service coverage—electricity, running water, and sewage—in the country. In 1992, only 2 percent had services in southern, Quechua-speaking sections of the city like San Luis Tasas, while only 3 percent were covered in northern Aymara neighborhoods like Villa Ingenio.[10] In 2001, 53 percent of households lacked running water, 80 percent lacked sewage, the rate of illiteracy was 10 percent, and the average income per family was $2 per day.[11]

Since waged employment was largely unavailable, El Alto's economy revolved almost entirely around informal, artisanal, commercial, and service activities. *Pluri-multi* reforms aside, in Bolivia ethnic discrimination limited possibilities for economic growth more than anywhere else in Latin America, according to the Inter-American Development Bank. The ruling MNR-MIR coalition's plan for "public works with jobs" would only add another $5 billion to the external debt and keep the party machine politics functioning, but do little to alleviate misery or outline a better future in El Alto or elsewhere.

While the weight of social movements had become evident, so had their limitations: political alliances were absent, there was considerable rivalry between the two popular *caudillos*, Quispe and Morales, and Olivera faded out of view (except internationally). In parliament, the new opposition forces were unable to make headway when faced with the ruling coalition's majority. Sánchez de Lozada's right-wing program—now, ironically, a continuation of Banzer's—was evident in his selection of "The Fox," Carlos Sánchez Berzaín, as Minister of the Presidency. When Sánchez de Lozada, aware of *cocalero* strength, at first proposed a temporary halt to coca eradication, George W. Bush's emissary to Bolivia, Otto Reich, effectively vetoed the measure, threatening to cut off US aid. As anticipated, coca growers mounted road blockades in protest, beginning in mid-January 2003. Quechua-speaking highland valley peasants from Potosí and Chuquisaca, 30,000 of whom marched on Sucre, joined the *cocaleros* of the Chapare and Yungas. Although the peasant trade union federation in La Paz was ready to blockade in solidarity, Quispe was pursuing negotiations with the government. Hence the Aymara tended to their harvests instead of taking over the roads. Morales and MAS saw that without practical support from Quispe and the CSUTCB/MIP, they had no chance of extracting concessions from Sánchez de Lozada, who insisted on an end to blockades and the re-imposition of "the principle of authority."

Then, on 12 February, a dramatic revolt took place in La Paz after the government issued a 12.5 percent, IMF-dictated income tax measure on salaries greater than $110/month, designed to reduce the budget deficit from 8.5 to 5.6 percent. In response to the announcement, the underpaid police force had gone into a work stoppage and retreated to its quarters on 11 February. The next day at noon, young people of Aymara descent—who had organized with the families of the police—stoned the unprotected Presidential Palace. Military Police and the Presidential Guard then turned out to open fire on police who had come to protest in the Plaza Murillo. Ten policemen and four military men died in the skirmish, and the spark of revolt spread. Crowds headed by young men torched the headquarters of the four major neoliberal political parties (MNR, MIR, ADN, UCS), the vice-president's office, the Ministry of Sustainable Development, the Ministry of Labor, and two important businesses. In El Alto, crowds led by young people set fire to the mayor's office and the electric and water companies. The military did little to stop the looting that accompanied the targeted political violence.

Old men and women, as well as children and adolescents of both sexes worked overnight in El Alto to defend their neighborhoods. By the morning of 13 February, with 13 people dead in La Paz and 5 in El Alto, there was popular fury over the senseless loss of life. Protesters bravely confronted lethal violence from snipers trying to hold the Plaza Murillo and soldiers trying to re-take El Alto, where demonstrators destroyed Bancosol (one of Sánchez de Lozada's neoliberal micro-credit schemes in the 1990s) and targeted Coca-Cola. By the afternoon of 13 February, 29 people had been killed and 205 had been injured by government troops, most of them just blocks from the Plaza Murillo. When the police returned to work that afternoon, they rounded up 180 suspects (one third of them minors). Sánchez de Lozada, who had fled the national palace in disguise, wildly alleged that the violence had been part of a coup attempt by MAS and the right-wing opposition party New Republican Force (NFR). The media focused on the looting and tagged the uprising a deplorable instance of juvenile delinquency. Thus was a precarious semblance of "order" restored to the capital, even as the destruction of the symbols of political authority spread briefly to Oruro and Santa Cruz.[12] Sánchez de Lozada dismissed his cabinet—except for the Minister of Defense and the Finance Minister, closely tied to the US Embassy and the IMF, respectively—and repealed the salary tax.

The revolt had shocked and frightened the urban middle and upper classes, and exposed to all the erosion of government control. The appointment of Sánchez Berzaín as Minister of Defense at the end of August, government claims about a "narco-terrorist conspiracy" spawning in the country, and the passage of the "Law of Citizen Security"—which penalized road blockades with sentences of up eight years—did not augur well for the conflicts that loomed in September. No one, however, anticipated that October would hold in store Bolivia's third major revolutionary moment.

10

Anatomy of an Uprising, 2003

Act One

The October 2003 insurrection that came to be known as the Gas War got its start inconspicuously in the La Paz countryside. On 27 July, the government detained Edwin Huampu on charges of murdering Elías Mamani (23) and Valentín Ramos (74). The latter two had been caught cattle rustling, and condemned to death in a community assembly in Cota Cota, an unusually extreme measure according to codes of communal justice. In calling the meeting and ratifying a course of action chosen by the majority, however, Huampu, the general secretary of the community's peasant trade union central, acted on orders from the sub-prefect of Pucarani, Manuel Cuevas, and in accordance with the precepts of community leadership.

Huampu was imprisoned in the San Pedro jail (formerly known as the Panopticon) in La Paz, and punished individually for what was, in essence, an act of public and collective violence sanctioned by the highest state authority in the jurisdiction. The incarceration of Huampu led to the collision of opposing conceptions of law and justice, and his ex-carceration was added to the list of Aymara peasant demands ratified in the Isla del Sol Accords in 2001. On 8 September, led by their *jilaqatas* and *mama t'allas* (traditional male authorities and their female consorts), 10,000 community members from Los Andes province joined with neighborhood associations in El Alto (FEJUVE), students from El Alto's public university (UPEA), and inter-provincial truckers to march from El Alto to Plaza San Francisco, and from there to Plaza San Pedro, where they protested in front of the prison and demanded Huampu's release.

Meanwhile, four hundred meters above in El Alto, the first of many civic strikes that would paralyze the city began in opposition to the proposed Maya and Paya plan. According to the regional workers' central (COR) and the FEJUVE, this would have given the mayor's office the necessary information about building and home construction to raise taxes on both. Amidst the wide array of groups represented and demands put forth, including public university autonomy and a rejection of the Free Trade Agreement of the Americas (FTAA), the common thread uniting protesters was a rejection of the planned export of Bolivian gas via Chile to California. This was an arrangement first conceived at the end of Sánchez de Lozada's previous term in 1997, which the successor ADN administration continued to negotiate behind closed doors with private gas companies. Now the social movements had gotten wind of the plan and roundly rejected it.

The following day, 9 September, the government failed to come to an agreement with Quispe and the CSUTCB, and its two negotiators were temporarily held hostage until a higher-level meeting was scheduled. The community leaders demanded the immediate release of Huampu and the abrogation of the law of "Citizen Protection and Security" that criminalized road blockades. They opposed the export of gas via Chile, and reminded the government of the unfulfilled promises contained in the 72 points of the Isla del Sol Accords. On 10 September, after another failure of negotiations, 1,000 Aymara community representatives led by Quispe, along with UPEA students and transport workers, initiated a hunger strike at Radio San Gabriel in El Alto, and called for blockades to begin immediately, threatening "civil war" in the face of government militarization of Aymara regions.

On 15 September, Aymara communities in Omasuyos began to blockade "in defense of gas," anticipating marches and protests to come, while FEJUVE and the COR shut down their city. In El Alto, there was no public transport, as blockades were set up in the principal artery leading south to Oruro, the Avenida 6 de Marzo. To the north, a series of blockades lined the Avenida Juan Pablo Segundo, the strongest of them at the far north in Río Seco. The roads through Villa Fátima leading out of La Paz to the east and the Yungas were cut off on the other side of the cordillera. The entire department, including the capital, was incommunicado, and the strikes continued on 16–17 September, with El Alto mobilized to block the imposition of the Maya and Paya plan. In Omasuyos and Los Andes, the roads were closed and under community control. On 18

September, Aymara peasants from the south marched on Mallasa, just outside La Paz, 11,000 in all.

On 19 September, the "*Coordinadora* for the Defense and Recuperation of Gas," led by Oscar Olivera, Evo Morales, and MAS, mobilized more than 50,000 in La Paz and 20,000 in Cochabamba to protest the proposed export of gas to Chile. As in April 2000, Olivera presided over open-air cabildos of tens of thousands—factory workers, coca growers from the Chapare, students, civic organizations, *regantes*—in the Plaza 14 de Septiembre in Cochabamba. The following day, Minister of Defense Carlos Sánchez Berzaín led the mission to "liberate" 800 tourists stranded in Sorata. This military operation left three Aymaras dead in Warisata and another in Ilabaya.

Throughout Omasuyos, using paths known only to them, their sheep and cattle, Aymara community members moved by night to avoid state authority, in a tactic they called *Plan Añutaya*, named after the small, fox-like nocturnal animal that "cares for the harvest" by eating pests. Once a consensus on the need to initiate a blockade was reached in Warisata with community representatives from several provinces in the department of La Paz, the word spread around the altiplano, on foot and via community radio stations broadcasting the decision four times daily in Aymara. Though Quispe and most of the hunger strikers remained in San Gabriel, leaders from Omasuyos returned home to organize. The mobilization grew, encompassing the southernmost province of La Paz, Aroma, where eleven were detained on 23 September. Along with Edwin Huampu, nine of the eleven were freed the next day, but two more leaders from Aroma became prisoners in San Pedro and another twenty-one were arrested. Quispe announced the end of all dialogue, since the demands for the demilitarization of Aymara territory, and negotiation in Warisata had not been met. Lettuce, tomatoes, radishes, and other vegetables were held up in the south of La Paz, and markets in La Paz closed on 23 September in memory of those massacred in Warisata. Prices would soon double. The Landless Workers' Movement—founded in Tarija in 2000 after the example of Brazilian rural workers and subsequently gaining ground in different parts of the country—called for land takeovers after 26 September. The coca growers in the Chapare announced blockades on the road from Santa Cruz to Cochabamba; and the COB announced a general strike for 30 September.

On 29 September, the demand for the president to resign circulated widely in the countryside via Aymara-language radio stations. In El Alto, butchers and transport workers went on strike and marched with market vendors' associations and UPEA students down to the Plaza San Francisco to join the COB, under its Executive Secretary Jaime Solares, for a public assembly. In El Alto, COR militants practiced *Plan Abeja*, stinging like bees at strategic points without maintaining a full blockade. The following day, 30 September, Oscar Olivera, the *Coordinadora*, and a group of 300 initiated a march to Warisata, and the COB's Solares ordered the implementation of daily blockades and marches.

On 1 October, most of the national-popular agenda was set: industrialization of gas and not its export through Chile; no to the FTAA; abrogation of the "Citizen Protection and Security" law; along with the resignation of the president. Permanent mobilization had begun. On 2 October, at the COB's assembly in the Plaza San Francisco, the multitude demanded the president's resignation. In El Alto, COR and UPEA students marched to meet with community hunger strikers at Radio San Gabriel, engaging in fierce combat with security forces on the Avenida 6 de Marzo that resulted in the arrest of twelve city residents (*alteños*). Most importantly, that day the Aymara peasantry—with coca, alcohol, and *aptapi* (communal feasting)—began the celebration that marks the beginning of the preparation of the soil for sowing, and put protest on hold. The insurgent momentum now passed to the city of El Alto, where women and youth took on unprecedented leadership roles.[1]

Act Two

On 8 October, the regional workers' central (COR) and neighborhood organizations (FEJUVE) in El Alto called a general strike against the export of gas. It counted on the solidarity of 800 miners from Huanuni, who were of particular symbolic significance given the role they had played in the National Revolution of 1952 and in recasting an anti-imperialist, national-popular tradition of resistance to the state after 1960. At the same time, it is striking to note that in 2003, many of the Huanuni miners mobilized affirming their own "indigenous" roots. When the police fired on them at Ventilla on 9 October, on the outskirts of El Alto, one became the latest martyr to fall "in defense of gas." Beginning in Warisata in September and spreading to El Alto in October, the mourning of martyrs provided a time to express grief and fury, to bolster the spirit through ritual and reflection, and to dedicate ongoing struggle to those who had lost their lives. The martyrs also provided a new example of indigenous patriotism in Bolivia, insofar as Aymaras were the ones defending the nation against foreign control. However, as the struggle counted on solidarity from miners and other sectors, it went from being an Aymara to a broader "popular" struggle led by Aymaras, rural and urban.

Combining the Aymara community tactic of surrounding the city from the countryside with street fighting reminiscent of earlier national-popular mobilizations, barricades went up throughout El Alto on 10 October. Protesters decided to cut the supply of gas to La Paz by surrounding the Senkata plant, property of what remained of the state petroleum company, YPFB. With helicopters circling above and tanks clattering through streets, eleven more were killed in the military operation that brought 37 cisterns of gas down to La Paz on 11 October.

The crisis intensified on 12 October—the anniversary of Columbus's incursion into the Americas. Massacres that day and the following one left fifty-four civilians martyred "in defense of gas." Insurgent urban Aymaras launched national-popular demands that were quickly taken up by other sectors: the call for the resignation of Sánchez de Lozada and his ministers; a trial for those responsible for the killing; the repeal of Sánchez de Lozada's 1996 Hydrocarbons Law privatizing gas resources; the rejection of the FTAA; and the convening of a constitutional assembly. The patriotic heroes from El Alto were warmly received by the residents of the northwestern hillside neighborhoods of La Paz as they marched down to Plaza San Francisco on 13 October, more than 100,000 strong. Overwhelmed and out of ammunition, police tendered white flags and withdrew as the Aymara-dominated multitude took over the city center. As the conflict in El Alto raged on, the uprising spread to Oruro, which called for a civic strike to begin on 14 October.

Evo Morales and Felipe Quispe were unable to provide representation or lead in La Paz and El Alto, much less at the national level. At the early stage of conflict in September, Minister of Government Yerko Kukoc claimed he could not negotiate in Warisata, Sorata, or Achacachi, because no one was in charge. In the climactic days of October, heterogeneous popular forces organized themselves, deliberated in open assemblies, and took action in their own spheres without waiting for orders from political party, trade-union, or other established leaders. The lack of centralized authority stymied government efforts to suppress the uprising, even by the application, in the Bolivian context, of extraordinary levels of lethal violence.

On 14 October, the mobilization spread to Oruro, Potosí, Sucre, Cochabamba, and Santa Cruz, toward which peasant colonizers marched from Yapacaní (lying to the north) and San Julián (to the east). The lowland region of Moxos, the former Jesuit mission district, was also closed. In Potosí, confederated *ayllus* shut down all the roads in the department, while Sucre was likewise impassable, except for the 25,000 who marched on the judicial capital and stoned the Supreme Court. The entire mining axis (Catavi, Siglo XX, and Huanuni) was blocked off. In Oruro, the city closest to the mining region, markets were closed, marches circulated around the central plaza, and university students clashed with security forces. In the region of Cochabamba, the *regantes* cut off the road to La Paz, while street fighting broke out in the city center, leaving nine people with bullet wounds. In the afternoon, 1,300 coca growers led by Dionisio Núñez arrived in La Paz from the Yungas, and it was expected that communities from Omasuyos would arrive in El Alto by nightfall.

Everything in La Paz was closed, and the civic committee went on strike demanding the president's resignation. The main arteries of the hillside neighborhoods of La Paz were blockaded, and the communities that surround the exclusive southern neighborhoods (*zona sur*) marched and blockaded. The mayor of La Paz, Juan del Granado, joined with the former Human Rights Omsbudswoman, Ana María Campero, and factions of the MIR and NFR to demand Goni's resignation. In El Alto, city residents mourned and buried their dead, but announced a march on the capital for 16 October, and under cover of darkness that night, thousands of men, women, and children took over a storage lot and, by hand, dragged train cars for several kilometers to the bridge where the highway from La Paz meets El Alto. Then they pushed the cars off the tracks. Not even tanks could get through.

The next morning, when they stopped for breakfast in Patacamaya, 2,500 miners from Huanuni were ambushed by soldiers, and two miners were killed while another—the mother of six children—was fatally wounded. The leader of the co-operative miners' union declared that all 50,000 of its members should prepare to march on La Paz.[2] The Mantego Regiment of Rangers (which hunted down Che Guevara in its glory days) was deployed in the wealthy *zona sur* of the capital to keep Aymaras from Chaskipampa out of the city. The President's spokesman alleged that Colombian and Peruvian guerrillas were behind the mobilizations, intending to install a "seditious and extremist" government. In the afternoon, led by Ana María Campero and other middle-class intellectuals and personalities, hunger strikes were set up in churches across the city, demanding the constitutional succession of Vice-President Carlos Mesa. General barracks went up throughout El Alto, and in District 5 near Río Seco, where the heaviest fighting occurred on 12–13 October, members of neighborhood associations attacked the military forces with dynamite. The city of Oruro remained under popular control, and peasants initiated blockades in much of the sparsely populated crossroads department, shutting down commerce with Chile on the western frontier. Popular forces controlled Sucre, Potosí, and Cochabamba, and the marches from San Julián and Yapacaní reached Santa Cruz.

Alteños marched again on 16 October, arriving at Plaza San Francisco via the three main routes into the capital. This time there were 300,000 protesters, including miners, community leaders from the provinces, students, housewives, telephone workers, taxi and bus drivers, market vendors, and child workers. More Aymaras arrived from the communities surrounding the exclusive *zona sur*: Ovejuyo, Mallasa, Río Abajo, while hunger strikers now numbered in the hundreds. A human chain of middle-class progressives was formed from San Miguel in the *zona sur* in order to reach hunger strikers 20 km away in Sopocachi. Hunger strikes then spread to Switzerland, Argentina, Peru, and Ecuador, where Bolivians in exile led protests that, in some cases, counted on broad progressive support. Expressions of solidarity poured in from civilians and popular organizations around the world.

In the eastern lowlands, although the police prevented marchers from entering Santa Cruz, indigenous groups mobilized as well. The Guaraní People's Assembly along with the Ayoreo, Guarayu, Chiquitano, Yuracaré, and the Moxeños added their energies to the hunger strike in solidarity with their highland brothers and sisters. In La Paz, Solares and the COB called a hunger strike of "the poor." Though US Ambassador David Greenlee and Goni held fast, the diplomatic representatives from Argentina and Brazil urged Sánchez de Lozada to resign, and Vice-President Mesa publicly distanced himself from the regime, leaving open the possibility of a constitutional succession. In the afternoon of the 16th, news arrived that the military had let the rest of the miners from Huanuni through the checkpoint at Patacamaya, and by evening, the *jilaqatas* and *mama t'allas* from Omasuyos—along with their armed commandos—reached El Alto. Though rumors of massacres and coups circulated, and random searches and arrests continued, the sense that Goni's days in Bolivia were over became ever more palpable.

Act Three

The insurrection gave rise to increasingly radical positions: "It was either us or him," as one *alteño* rebel put it. "There was nothing else to do, Mr Journalist . . . We were going for his head, to take him from the palace by force."[3] Yet in the end, the October insurrectionists did not attempt to seize the state administration, and instead set up alternative institutions for self-government in city streets and neighborhoods of La Paz and El Alto, and in the insurgent highlands of Sorata, Warisata, and Achacachi. Protesters, who took over the downtown center, intentionally refrained from marching on the national palace.[4] This was to avoid bloodshed, but it was also a recognition that substantial power was already in their hands. No longer was the city under siege, or surrounded, as in 1781—it had been effectively taken over and occupied. It was now only the national palace and congress, with a cordon of a few blocks around it, that remained under de facto "state" control.

On 17 October—with increasing numbers of protesters pouring into the El Alto and yet more setting out from the countryside to march on the capital, and with security forces unwilling to suppress the populace— a bitter Sánchez de Lozada was forced to resign and retreat. Only his immediate family, his most draconian ministers, and the US Embassy were still behind him by the time he boarded his flight to Miami. Carlos Mesa assumed power that evening with no political apparatus of his own and an October agenda imposed upon him by mobilized popular forces. In his formal address to the nation, he acknowledged his three tasks in office: to repeal the existing Hydrocarbons Law; to hold a popular refer- endum on the future of hydrocarbon resources and development; and to hold a new constitutional assembly. In a subsequent speech to assembled crowds in the Plaza San Francisco, he said: "If I don't follow through, you can kick me out."

11

Interregnum, 2003–5

The Center Does Not Hold

Carlos Mesa lacked any political experience whatsoever prior to the electoral campaign of 2002. He was known as a sober television news personality from a prominent intellectual family in La Paz, and as the author of books on Bolivian film and history—including one study of the country's republican presidents. Politically independent yet an admirer of Sánchez de Lozada's neoliberal reforms in the mid–1990s, he was chosen as a running mate by Sánchez de Lozada to appeal to unaligned middle classes. When he donned the presidential sash himself, he enjoyed high levels of popularity in opinion polls, given his status as political outsider, lack of a clearly defined constituency, and refusal to sanction the massacre in Black October. The social movements treated him skeptically, yet granted him an initial measure of time in which to carry out his mandate.

Mesa put together a cabinet composed of progressive intellectuals (Interior, Indigenous Affairs) and neoliberal technocrats (Finance, Hydrocarbons), a formula that had worked during Sánchez de Lozada's first term. At the same time, Mesa had no party-clientelist machine to offset the hostility of the traditional parties in congress or to set in motion in moments of acute confrontation. The underlying political support for his administration came instead from a tacit alliance with Evo Morales and MAS. Morales used the bargain to obtain a strong hand in shaping government decisions—such as a halt in coca eradication—and to organize— in the virtual absence of contending parties—for the municipal elections in 2004 and in anticipation of the constitutional assembly.

Across the country there was vigorous popular debate in anticipation of the binding referendum on gas held on 18 July 2004, and over the possibility of nationalizing hydrocarbons. The referendum was one of the achievements of the October insurrection, yet the Mesa government refused to make nationalization an option for voters and designed the referendum to sidestep the issue. According to the government's in-house polls, a great majority favored nationalization, yet the Mesa administration maintained it was financially and technically unviable and would shut the door on future foreign investment. Many key organizations (COB, CSUTCB, COR-El Alto, FEJUVE, the *Coordinadora* for the Defense and Recuperation of Gas), calling for abrogation of the contracts signed with multinationals under Sánchez de Lozada's Hydrocarbons Decree, ultimately boycotted the referendum on the grounds that it would not be the exercise in direct democracy it was intended to be.

The five questions of the referendum were as follows: 1. Do you agree that the current Hydrocarbons Law should be changed? 2. Do you agree that the Bolivian state should have rights to hydrocarbons once they are extracted from the ground? 3. Do you agree that YFPB should be re-established in order to control hydrocarbon production? 4. Do you agree that Bolivian gas should be used to regain useful or sovereign access to the Pacific? 5. Do you agree that Bolivian gas should be exported, and that multinationals should pay 50 percent of projected profits for rights to exploit Bolivian gas, and that the government should invest in health, education, and infrastructure? Both Mesa and Morales proclaimed the referendum a victory for participatory democracy, though the abstention rate was 40 percent. Morales and MAS had urged the movements to vote yes on the first three questions and no on the last two. While a majority voted yes on all five questions, the last two received less than half of the total votes, since more people handed in blank or null ballots than voted yes. Yet the government obtained the response from the electorate that it had carefully prepared: Sánchez de Lozada's hydrocarbon law would be repealed, while a balance would be struck between popular demands and the property rights and profit rates of multinational capital. Mesa's stance on nationalization—or rather his deliberate avoidance of the issue— finally brought the regime into open confrontation with the popular political organizations that supported the October insurrection and brought it into being in the first place.

The traditional parties remained discredited and in disarray. Their obstructionist position towards the October Agenda had proven ineffective, and none was able to make an impressive showing in the municipal elections in December 2004. The main faction of the MNR overcame its initial shock to regroup around Sánchez de Lozada, yet was hampered by internal dissent. The MIR had fragmented, NFR had little profile, and ADN had virtually dissolved (though "Tuto" Quiroga remained the one traditional politician with future electoral prospects).

In contrast to Ecuador and Venezuela, Bolivia's armed forces steered clear of direct involvement in politics. While pro-American and pro-Chávez tendencies coexisted uneasily, neither was willing or able to act on its own in order to bring about a coup. The US government reluctantly came around to accepting Mesa and the Hydrocarbons Law in the expectation that he would contain popular pressure for more immediate, radical change. The Andean region as a whole has become a growing source of concern, though in South America, the US was chiefly preoccupied with overthrowing Chávez in Venezuela and fortifying Uribe in Colombia. It held back from more overt intervention in Bolivia, perhaps betting that the political process would exhaust itself before the radical agenda—including nationalization of hydrocarbons and challenges to its coca eradication policies—advanced any further.

Despite the weakness of its rivals in the 2004 municipal elections, MAS garnered only 18 percent of the vote nationwide; its only significant urban showing was in Cochabamba, which it did not win. Quispe's MIP was all but absent, and ad hoc coalitions of "citizen groups"—front groups for politicians recycled from the neoliberal parties—were the only clear winners, while incumbent mayors held onto their posts. With the elections past and with popular resentment mounting over Mesa's deceptive handling of the new hydrocarbons initiative and his diffidence toward the October Agenda, MAS finally withdrew from its awkward marriage of convenience with Mesa.

In 2005, political polarization grew dramatically along racial-ethnic, class, and regional lines. Following the announcement of price hikes on gas and diesel, in mid-January, FEJUVE won what was immediately branded "the Second Water War," as a three-day civic strike led to the abrogation of El Alto's and La Paz's contract with Aguas de Illimani (a subsidiary of the French multinational Suez).[1] Unlike October, protesters did not face the concentrated state violence that had previously brought the middle class into the streets, and in La Paz, a fraction of the middle class tied to the administration and residents from Mesa's neighborhood turned out to protest *against* popular mobilization. Mesa defended water and petroleum multinationals rhetorically, but did not send tanks into the streets. After FEJUVE successfully challenged Aguas de Illimani and Mesa's government, debate on the Hydrocarbons Law began in the Lower House of Congress.

The Shape of Reaction

Entrepreneurial elites in Santa Cruz and Tarija responded with furious reaction, which they had rehearsed since October, as they joined with the ruling classes in Beni and Pando to form the "half moon" (*la media luna*) territorial bloc in the eastern and southeastern lowlands. They drew from longstanding and widespread regionalist sentiment against centralized authority in La Paz—ironically, given the disproportionate amount of central government subsidies that Santa Cruz received from the 1950s through the 1970s—as well as racist scorn of highland Indians. While the breadth of support for the regional civic committees is often exaggerated, at the regional level their influence over government and what remains of the political party establishment is significant.

In January 2005, the Santa Cruz Civic Committee led a successful crusade for autonomy in the department with the nation's second-largest gas reserves. As a result of three weeks of civic strikes like those employed during the UDP period, they forced Mesa to grant a referendum on regional autonomy. The civic committee in Tarija, where Bolivia's largest gas reserves are located, clamored for a similar agreement. This put the question of regional and municipal autonomy, which was to be addressed in the constitutional assembly, on the negotiating table. Along with national sovereignty, autonomy was a demand shared by peasant colonizers, most of Quechua-Aymara descent, and lowland indigenous groups, but their views about autonomy were directly opposed to those of the civic committees. The former had been part of the national-popular bloc in formation in October, whereas the autonomy favored by the latter was designed to forestall the coalescence of such a bloc.

The Santa Cruz Civic Committee's concerns revolved around the threat posed to foreign investment and private property by the draft of the Hydrocarbons Law and the expulsion of Aguas del Illimani. *Cruceño* leaders talked of launching a separatist civil war (with strong racialist connotations) if the Hydrocarbons Law was passed *tel quel*. Mass mobilization from the left, centered in El Alto, thus led to mass mobilization from the right, grounded in Santa Cruz. In response, Mesa gave support to the prefect of Santa Cruz, dropped what little remained of his progressive veneer, and moved to a more full-throated defense of oil-gas and water multinationals, which translated into a discursive attack on social movements and their leaders. Mesa cleansed his cabinet of progressive ministers and stacked it with neoliberals favorably disposed to the multinational, as opposed to the October, agenda.

With the "January Agenda," the regionalist right, acting as the voice of local business interests allied to foreign capital, won its first real political victory since the re-election of Sánchez de Lozada in 2002. The main thing now distinguishing Mesa from Goni was the former's unwillingness to shed innocent blood to hold on to office. Though a partial gain had been achieved by the national-popular forces in mid-January, Mesa dragged his feet on setting a date of departure for Aguas de Illimani. Demanding that the company be turned over immediately to a reconstituted SAMAPA (the public enterprise that ran the water and sewage system before 1997), FEJUVE struck again on 2 March, and three days later, Morales and Olivera announced forthcoming marches and blockades in solidarity with the *alteño* movement for national sovereignty over natural resources.

After Mesa broke with MAS over its support for direct action as a means of influencing the outcome of parliamentary debate on the Hydrocarbons Law, the beleaguered President called the country ungovernable, and threatened to resign on 6 March 2005. As blockades spread to the Yungas, Potosí, Chuquisaca, and Oruro, and intensified in El Alto and the Chapare, the traditional parties, previously resentful of Mesa's autonomy and popularity, rallied to his defense in the name of "democratic" governance. Having lost his fragile base on the center-left, Mesa had little choice but to embrace the right in order to stay in power.

The convergence of Mesa with the right, and the loss of middle-class support for a new national-popular project, was offset by a tendency, however fragile and incipient, toward greater programmatic unity among the normally divided movement leaders. This was demonstrated by a meeting at COB headquarters in La Paz on 9 March. This was a coming together, for the first time, of leaders of the COB; both the Morales and Quispe wings of the divided CSUTCB; Olivera, heading up a revived *Coordinadora* in Defense of Water and Gas; leaders of the landless peasants' union (MST); and even Morales and Quispe themselves. Only FEJUVE, suspicious of parties and *caudillos*, abstained from the "Pact for Unity."

The national-popular bloc whose outlines first appeared in October had taken over center stage once again, shutting down seven of nine departments and sealing off most cities. When a new version of the Hydrocarbons Law—which would increase government revenue from the current level of $150 million to $600 million annually—passed from the House to the Senate, on 15 March, Mesa complained of being "blockaded in Congress and blockaded in the streets." He therefore announced his intention to call elections before his term ended in August 2007.

The measure was declared unconstitutional by the courts, and though the new Hydrocarbons Law would not raise revenues to levels demanded by the social movements—much less nationalize the industry—its passage from House to Senate was enough to pull Morales and MAS back into the parliamentary fold, thereby bringing blockades to an abrupt halt on 16 March. Had Morales abandoned Mesa, the government might well have fallen, emboldening national-popular forces to press for deeper changes in relation to the state and multinational capital. Yet without Mesa, and in the absence of a fully articulated national-popular bloc, a right-wing reaction could have ended Morales's presidential hopes, and disarticulated insurgent movements.

The June Insurrection

With right-wing elites based in the lowlands gaining greater purchase over the government, and with popular forces in the highlands seeking more progressive hydrocarbons legislation, executive power came under further strain and polarization as insurgency burst forth again in May and June of 2005. The latest uprising appeared to be a sequel to the insurrection of October 2003, with the mobilization of similar sectors, deploying similar tactics, leading to similar scenes in the streets of the capital.

The insurgency got underway in mid-May as FEJUVE and the COR declared an indefinite general strike in El Alto, and the CSUTCB, under the leadership of Román Loayza (MAS), mobilized communities in the provinces to pressure the senate over hydrocarbons legislation. Within two weeks, the marches and strikes that paralyzed the capital and El Alto had spread to Sucre, Potosí, and Cochabamba. Road blockades, meanwhile, shut down eight of Bolivia's nine departments by 6 June. Protesters' demands were various and shifting: many insisted on the constitutional assembly and a human rights trial for Sánchez de Lozada's state violence in October 2003; some voices called for Mesa's resignation, others for the closure of parliament. The most vigorous demand, however, was for nationalization of hydrocarbons.

For the reactionary bloc, whose most visible political leader was Hormando Vaca Diez (MIR), President of the Senate, the insurgency was double-edged. On one hand, the mobilizations had the desirable effect of further weakening Mesa, who was still beholden to the "October Agenda." If Mesa fell, executive power would pass directly into the hands of Vaca Diez, as head of the legislative branch. On the other hand, lowland elites were firmly set against protesters' demands for nationalization and the constitutional assembly. Pursuing the "January Agenda" of greater regional autonomy, their leaders insisted first and foremost on elections for departmental prefects, and refused the obvious compromise of holding simultaneous elections for delegates to the constitutional assembly as well as for departmental prefects. Instead, Vaca Diez resorted to stalling tactics in congress, hoping for Mesa's collapse, while risking heightened hostility on the part of the populace.

With his authority buckling, Mesa was prepared to bow out gracefully, asking the Catholic Church to intervene on 4–5 June in support of early elections. Turning its back on protesters, the Church pursued a settlement among political elites. Morales went along, subordinating non-violent direct action to electoral strategy, and positioning himself as a leading presidential candidate. Early elections would require that Mesa resign, and that Vaca Diez, followed by Mario Cossio (MNR), head of the Lower House, renounce his right to succeed to the presidency. Vaca Diez, however, refused to compromise, and the Church failed embarrassingly in its mission as political mediator.

Then, on 6 June 2005, between 400,000 and 500,000 protesters, overwhelmingly of Aymara descent, poured down from El Alto into the heart of the capital. Some twenty truckloads of community peasants from Aroma—home to Tupaj Katari and Pablo Zárate Villca—a province in La Paz on the high plains bordering the department of Oruro, arrived with clubs, stones, and slings. They were accompanied by neighborhood residents, rural and urban teachers, bakers, butchers, market women, street vendors, high-school and university students, factory workers, the unemployed, landless peasants, street kids, and community members from the countryside around La Paz, who pronounced unanimously in favor of nationalizing hydrocarbons. Miners announced their presence by setting off potent charges of dynamite. This was the largest wave of mobilization since October 2003, and it kept La Paz shut down for two weeks running. Crowds overflowed the Plaza San Francisco, and then headed off to the Plaza Murillo vowing to take over parliament and occupy the presidential palace.

At the end of the day, President Mesa offered his resignation. Nevertheless, protests continued to spread on 7–8 June: road blockades nearly doubled from 61 to 119, and in the lowlands, frontier settlers and Guaraní communities occupied seven gas fields owned by two petroleum multinationals, BP-Amoco and Repsol YPF. Three hydroelectric plants were also taken over, while in Tapacarí, Cochabamba, community peasants shut down pipeline valves—property of Transredes (Enron-Shell)—that carried 20,000 barrels of gas per day to Chile. The middle classes finally intervened as well. Led by mayors of the capital cities, nearly 100 hunger strikes took place in seven of nine departments, with more than 700 mostly middle-class people demanding nationalization, the resignation of Hormando Vaca Diez, and the convening of elections.

Finally, on 9 June, national-popular forces handed the reactionary bloc its second major defeat. Vaca Diez had transferred the session of Congress to Sucre, fleeing the siege in La Paz. Yet tens of thousands of miners and community peasants from Chuquisaca, Potosí, and Oruro quickly converged on the Plaza 25 de Mayo in Sucre in order to prevent Vaca Diez from succeeding Mesa. Stranded in Sucre by the airport workers' strike and under military custody to protect his life, Vaca Diez finally conceded, as did Cossio, the head of the Lower House. Close to midnight, Eduardo Rodríguez Veltzé, President of the Supreme Court, was finally sworn in as President. Rodríguez immediately called general elections for December, and national-popular forces demobilized on 12 June. Through direct action, insurgents had forced Vaca Diez to step aside.

In October 2003, after peasants from the La Paz countryside initiated the process, FEJUVE and the COR came to spearhead the insurrection, with miners playing a secondary role. In June 2005, FEJUVE and the COR kicked things off, but miners and the CSUTCB carried the process to its national culmination. Culturally and politically, however, miners and peasants had few possibilities of building bridges to the urban middle class. In fact, without the unifying element of state violence, ties between progressive middle-class groups and other popular forces were more tension-filled in June 2005 than they had been in October 2003. In June 2005, reactionary sectors of the middle class, supported by the MNR and MIR, organized "self-defense" militias in La Paz. A progressive middle-class fraction ultimately joined the national-popular movement, yet its action came even later than in October 2003.

If the latest uprising bore a strong resemblance to that of October 2003, direct action was even broader in geographical scope the second time around. Nationalization had also acquired far greater resonance than before. Yet the outcome was ultimately even more mixed, with gains and losses on both sides. Popular forces had demonstrated their growing strength, advanced the project for nationalization, and blocked Vaca Diez's bid for power. Yet the right had come within a hair's breadth of retaking the executive branch, and it effectively set the October Agenda back. There was no longer a president accountable to national-popular demands in office. Rodríguez Veltzé entered as an interim caretaker, with no political vision or mandate. Despite enormous sacrifices on the part of popular sectors, the accumulated popular energies would be dispersed at least temporarily. In the interim, the formal electoral process would allow the political elite time to regroup.

Triumph as Closure,
December 2005–August 2006

Landslide

The stunning victory of Evo Morales and MAS in the Bolivian presidential and legislative elections on 18 December 2005 opened a new phase in the political cycle that began in 2000. Morales himself proclaimed the outcome momentous: "A new history of Bolivia begins . . . We have an enormous responsibility to change our history."[1] For the international community, this came at a crucial time, at the start of an electoral cycle throughout Latin America in which the left was poised to make major gains. The question abroad was whether Morales's government would follow the Lula or the Chávez path—willing accommodation to global capital, or robust populist reformism allied to Cuban anti-imperialism. The question tended to ignore the distinctiveness of Bolivia's historical trajectory and political traditions. These domestic dynamics had determined the October Agenda that Morales was elected to implement.

Morales called the electoral outcome a "democratic revolution, a cultural revolution . . . with votes, not bullets," while connecting it to earlier cycles of historical insurgency—"as Tupac Katari said, we will return as millions."[2] Ironically enough, however, Morales's government would bring the current revolutionary cycle to a provisional close.

The MAS partially fulfilled the major demands of the "October Agenda," especially nationalization and the constitutional assembly, by quickening the administrative pace and centralizing power at the highest levels of the executive (president, vice-president, ministers of government and the presidency). This, in turn, demobilized and fragmented the movements that brought MAS to power. In order to assure the state's ability to govern, it at the same time granted significant concessions to the regionalist right in the south and southeast, a weakened political force that suffered major setbacks in the elections of December 2005 and July 2006. The specific government measures adopted by mid-2006—the nationalization of hydrocarbons, agrarian reform, and the constitutional assembly—and the closure of the revolutionary cycle, must be understood in another way as well. While the MAS reforms represent a response to the popular mandate, they are also a bid for state hegemony, intended to consolidate the medium-term governing plans of the MAS—just as the MNR stabilized its regime in the aftermath of popular insurrection of 1952.

Time Change

When Rodríguez Veltzé called for elections, Jorge "Tuto" Quiroga's new conservative coalition PODEMOS was the front runner. It was followed in the polls by the new National Unity (UN) party led by Samuel Doria Medina, a businessman known as the "king of cement" who had broken away from Jaime Paz Zamora and the now nearly defunct MIR. MAS was a contender, but polls were discouraging and skepticism was rife. Morales and his retinue had proven themselves as forces of political opposition, but were still outmanned in the halls of congress, and inexperienced in wielding the tools of state power. Few thought MAS capable of administering executive authority even if it were to overcome its persistent associations with political instability in the eyes of middle-class voters. Even among progressive sympathizers, the prospect of a MAS government under siege from the traditional oligarchic parties, the US Embassy, multinational corporations, and international financial institutions seemed a truly nightmarish scenario. Fearful memories of the UDP debacle in the early 1980s resurfaced, and many on the left thought it preferable for MAS to bide its time while "Tuto" Quiroga sustained the inevitable blows of the political melee.

The returns from the election thus came as a shock to all. It would be hard to exaggerate the significance of December's result, as Morales was one of the rare Bolivian presidents ever to have been accorded an absolute majority. Only Paz Estenssoro—following the national revolution of 1952—came to power with a similar degree of popular legitimacy and mandate for change. Whereas successful Bolivian presidential candidates usually scored below 25 percent of the popular vote, Morales and his vice-president Alvaro García Linera won 54 percent on a turnout of 85 percent. They carried all the cities except Santa Cruz, and even took 33 percent to the right's 42 percent in Santa Cruz Department, thanks in large part to García Linera's months of high-profile campaigning there, and despite the disqualification of hundreds of thousands of voters on a technicality. Though MAS had a bare majority in the Chamber of Deputies, having won 65 out of 130 seats in December, it had only 12 Senate seats out of 27. "Tuto" Quiroga's PODEMOS had 13 seats, and the MNR but one—its electoral collapse being another significant outcome of the polls.

Given initial expectations, the right did poorly overall, though not at the regional level. It took six of the nine departmental prefectures (comparable to state governors' mansions in the US) including not only Santa Cruz but Cochabamba and La Paz; MAS held only Oruro, Potosí, and Chuquisaca. Regionalist resistance to central government initiatives was one of the obstacles for the new government, although Evo's early popularity offset some of the pressure.

In the only country in the western hemisphere in which the bulk of the population identifies itself as indigenous, Morales was the first indigenous head of state. Born in 1959 in a rural area of a heavily Aymara region—Sur Carangas province in the department of Oruro—four of Morales's seven brothers died young as a result of the poverty and conditions in which they lived. Morales spent his childhood learning soccer with a ball made of rags while herding llamas in the hills; as they pastured, he would zigzag between them. His first job, at age four or five, was selling popsicles in northern Argentina (Jujuy) while his father looked for seasonal work as a cane-cutter. Because of difficulties with Spanish, Morales had to leave his first school near the cane fields. He remembers watching buses pass by as he walked the highways, marveling at people who threw orange and banana peels out the window. Collecting the scraps to eat, Morales aspired to ride a bus one day. Back in his community in Orinoca, he attended a local school and excelled at soccer, founding a team when he was thirteen. At sixteen, the three *ayllus* that composed Orinoca elected him to coach the selection for the entire canton, and with his father's help, Morales sold lamb and llama wool to buy balls and uniforms. To complete high school, he worked as a baker and bricklayer in Oruro before getting a job as a trumpet player with the Banda Real Imperial, one of Bolivia's most important brass bands.

By the time drought devastated the altiplano in 1982–3, Morales had already migrated to the Chapare with his family, and as a result of his athletic prowess, he was elected Sports Secretary for the San Francisco coca growers' trade union, one of six unions to make up the Tropical Federation in the region. Just four years later he became General Secretary, and by 1988, though not yet thirty, he was elected General Secretary of the Tropical Federation of coca growers.[3] By 1996, he had been elected General Secretary of the Six Tropical Federations, and the following year he was elected to Congress. The young leader worked his way up the ladder of posts in the country's only trade union to survive the neoliberal onslaught. The coca growers' movement was strengthened by the great migration that began with the drought in 1982–3, and the subsequent neoliberal crisis. The *cocaleros* were the only popular political movement to make it through the 1990s not only intact, but with direct political representation through Morales, elected to Congress in 1997.

Though growers stressed their connection to a millenarian culture of chewing "*la hoja sagrada*" (the sacred leaf), differentiating the coca leaf from cocaine, their political culture was a fusion of new lowland community and older trade union politics. It built on the strengths of the national-popular tradition of mining syndicalism in the highlands, but also brought a rural, communal dimension to the new environment. This was not conceived principally in ethnic terms; in fact, the coca growers' movement was remarkable for its anti-imperial and class identity.

Morales began to foreground his indigenous identity in the face of competition from Felipe Quispe's radical *indianismo*, after the Aymara blockades of 2000. In the 2002 elections, Morales appealed to Quispe's Aymara base, while relying on brother Ivan's hegemony over rural trade unions and indigenous communities in the Oruro highlands. Given the resurgence of Aymara trade union and community politics in the countryside and neighborhood associations in the city after 2000, it made sense for Morales to reach out to mobilized sectors beyond his stronghold in the lowland coca-growing regions. He did so with extraordinary success, but his conquest of the progressive middle-class vote was equally impressive.

Alvaro García Linera, the MAS vice-president, was the country's leading public intellectual, and his trajectory was similarly meteoric. He was born into a middle-class creole family in Cochabamba in 1962 and radicalized in high school under the Banzer dictatorship. As a student at UNAM in Mexico City, 1981–5, García Linera was closely involved in solidarity work against the Reagan-backed counterinsurgencies in Central America. Returning to Bolivia, he worked with revolutionary tin miners in the Cédulas Mineras de Base in northern Potosí. This group later fused with the "red *ayllu*" wing of the high-plains Aymara peasant movement, forming the EGTK, one of Latin America's few indigenous-led guerrilla forces, in 1990.

His first book was a theoretical polemic on nationalism and what Peruvian Marxist José Carlos Mariátegui called "the Indian question." It was published in 1989 under the *nom de guerre* Qananchiri (Aymara for "Clarifying Light"). Using the same pseudonym, in 1991 he published another Marxist theoretical treatise. Captured that year together with Felipe Quispe, García Linera was held indefinitely in Chonchocoro Maximum Security Prison on charges of armed uprising.[4] After an activist campaign secured the release of EGTK militants in 1997, García Linera found a post teaching sociology at the Universidad Mayor de San Andrés in La Paz, and wrote several books on the history and present condition of the Bolivian working class. He was a founding member of the radical intellectual collective "Comuna" in La Paz, contributing a stream of essays to their edited volumes, along with a torrent of articles for newspapers, magazines, and scholarly journals. A creative interpreter of Pierre Bourdieu, García Linera became the leading theorist of Bolivia's rising indigenous rural and working-class movements.[5]

Following the 2002 elections, García Linera's contributions on radio and especially television helped redefine the terms of national debate to reflect the new centrality of these currents and their demands. As a creole who had taken up arms with the Aymara guerrilla, suffered imprisonment yet not reneged, he acquired prestige and legitimacy in the eyes of many in popular movements. Beginning in spring 2003, he advocated a "social pact" to resurrect a national capitalist model of development, decolonize the state, and redistribute wealth and resources. When, in the summer of 2005, Morales and his advisors invited him to stand as vice-presidential candidate for MAS, of which he was not a member, he asked that the social movements be given time to express their views, rather than agreeing to a top-down *caudillo* arrangement.

Despite his background as an analyst of independent social movements, as the government's principal ideologue, García Linera recast Bolivia's new political forces in terms of "*Evismo*," thereby feeding into stereotypes about personalistic, populist power. In the July 2006 elections, the campaign slogan used by Morales and MAS—"*Evo soy yo*" (I am Evo)—followed a predictable script, banking on Morales's status as a charismatic popular leader or *caudillo*. What makes this contradictory is the contrast with Morales's use of Zapatista rhetoric indicating an ethos of service: "For us it's a question of leading by obeying the people."[6] As we have seen, there is truth to the statement insofar as Morales and MAS tail-ended, rather than led, the insurrections of 2003 and 2005.

In the electoral arena, it is true that Morales and MAS have served as the only effective vehicle for national articulation of the heterogeneous social movements. This was in fact MAS's original reason for being, and in retrospect the strategy looks ingenious. In the early 1990s, the coca growers and other peasant trade union leaders were aware of their grassroots and local potential, yet faced with the difficulty of converting isolated and intermittent strength into enduring political advantage. With left parties broken and disoriented, the idea was to construct a new "political instrument" for popular forces. When its early Political Instrument for the Sovereignty of the People moniker proved inviable for legal reasons, it borrowed the "Movement to Socialism" name from a left party on the verge of folding. Despite its revolutionary discourse, it began tentatively running candidates in presidential elections in the mid-1990s, though to little profit. The secret to its success was a turn to municipal elections in the Chapare, which MAS began to sweep with unheard-of levels of support. In 1998, Evo Morales ran as a uninominal candidate for congress (representing a local Chapare district), receiving the highest percentage of any congressional candidate in history.

MAS featured peasant trade-unionists, indigenous activists, veteran leftists of all stripes, and independent intellectuals among its ranks. But MAS is largely a coalition of personalist factions, with that of Morales exercising unquestioned supremacy; it has none of the bureaucratic infrastructure of the Brazilian Workers' Party, for example. MAS really broke through onto the national stage only in 2002. Hence the inexperience of its cadres and administrators cannot be overemphasized, and likewise the influence of unelected advisors.[7] Nonetheless, MAS surprised one and all as it quickly centralized power after January 2006 and made headway on a set of key reforms.

Nationalization

No one—least of all Morales and García Linera—claimed electoral victory would fundamentally alter capitalist relations of property and production. It was expected to modify the rules of neoliberal capitalism in favor of a state that would work to improve the welfare of *all* its citizens, especially the poor rural and urban indigenous majority, through redistributive policies and social programs. Before Mesa's overthrow in 2005, in which nationalization was the unifying demand, and after Sánchez de Lozada's exit in 2003, 92 percent of voters in Bolivia's "gas referendum" of July 2004 indicated support for nationalization, although the referendum intentionally avoided using the term. What, exactly, was meant by nationalization varied according to movement, party, regional, ethnic, and class affiliations. In other words, cleavages dividing Bolivian society were expressed through debates over natural gas exploitation.

Associated with the national-popular tradition, Morales chose May Day to nationalize hydrocarbons with Supreme Decree 28701, "Heroes of the Chaco War Decree," in Bolivia's largest gas field, San Alberto, in Caraparí, Tarija. Once more, Morales alluded to the long tradition of resource extraction he had been elected to reverse: "For more than 500 years, our resources have been pillaged," Morales declared. "This has to end now." In name, Decree 28701 enshrined the official foundational moment of the national-popular—the Chaco War—and Morales made explicit reference to both indigenous insurgency and national-popular struggle:

> We express to Bolivia and the world . . . that the struggle of our ancestors like Tupac Katari, Tupac Amaru, Bartolina Sisa . . . were not in vain. Today we dignify the sacrifice of our grandfathers who went to the Chaco War to defend our natural resources, the participation of the armed forces in the nationalizations of 1937 and 1969, together with Marcelo Quiroga Santa Cruz.[8]

In a move designed to cement ties with the military—one of the great enemies at times, but also great allies of past national-popular projects—Morales then sent troops to "protect" the country's two largest gas fields (San Alberto and San Antonio).

Soldiers departed soon after the cameras, but the major demand of the insurrection of June 2005 had now become official government policy. Foreign and domestic left critiques of the favorable conditions afforded the multinationals were quickly forthcoming and factually well-grounded, yet they carried little weight in Bolivian debate.[9] In effect, they missed the point: in contrast to previous governments, Morales could plausibly claim, "We are not a government of promises. We respect and we comply with what we propose and what the Bolivian people ask for."[10] It is easy to dismiss the ceremony and concrete reform policies, no matter how tepid, of the "Third Nationalization" as so many theatrics. Yet this risks ignoring deeply held popular convictions. The Morales-García Linera government has deliberately sought to mobilize myths, symbols, and memories associated with a radical past in order to consolidate power and attain lasting legitimacy.

Fine Print

The "Heroes of the Chaco War Decree" represented a partial break with the neoliberal past, though it did not go so far as earlier nationalizations in Bolivian history. It claimed to "recover property, possession, and total and absolute control" over hydrocarbons, in keeping with the July 2004 popular referendum, but it did not mandate expropriation or abrogate contracts, which distinguished it from more radical nationalizations in 1937 and 1969. It opened up the possibility for more advantageous negotiations with multinational energy corporations, which were given six months for the "migration" of contracts signed under the law enacted by Sánchez de Lozada. In this respect, the new decree reaffirmed legislation approved but not implemented under Mesa, marking continuity rather than rupture. The Constitutional Court ruled that since Congress had not approved the terms set by Sánchez de Lozada, contracts signed on those terms were unconstitutional. In this as in other respects, the new decree stayed within constitutional limits.

The MAS decree aimed to reconstitute YPFB and establish a leading role for government in all aspects of the industry, from exploration to commercialization. After a thorough auditing of the public and private interests involved, it demanded transparent accounting of future costs, investments, and profits. The decree called for extending public control and ownership over oil and liquid national gas in the five public-private companies—Transredes (Shell-Enron subsidiary), Andina (Repsol), Chaco (BP-Amaco), ERP (Petrobras), and CLHB (German/Peruvian)—that once belonged entirely to the state. YPFB had controlled between 30 and 48 percent in the first three. Now the five firms were meant to participate in joint ventures in which YPFB has a controlling interest, which it would obtain through buy-backs and renegotiation of contracts to obtain at least 51 percent of their shares.

Most controversially for international business observers, the decree temporarily raised royalties on the two largest gas fields operating at capacity (San Antonio and San Alberto) from 50 percent to 82 percent. The two fields accounted for half of all production and 70 percent of exports, with each yielding over 100 million barrels per day.[11] Finally, prices and output for the domestic market were to be set by the Bolivian government, though exports remained subject to international price mechanisms, a delicate subject for negotiation with Argentina and Brazil.

Even if the decree fails to achieve its goals of increasing government revenues from $177 million to $780 million annually, in accordance with García Linera's calculations, initial developments went in favor of the government. Protest and mobilization from the left against the weakness of the decree failed to materialize. The reaction from governments (Brazil, Spain, US) and petroleum firms (Petrobras, Repsol, BP-Amoco, Shell-Enron) was initially fairly muted as well. In Argentina, Kirchner was willing to settle for higher gas prices, hitherto purchased at below-market rates. Although Lula came under increasing pressure in Brazil, with the semi-autonomous Petrobras taking a stand against the Bolivian measures, he was reluctant to come out against the measure.[12] This even in spite of a tight election race against a conservative candidate, Petrobras's $1.5 billion in investments, and the fact that one half of the gas consumed in Brazil came from Bolivia. Without it, Sao Paulo, the financial capital of South America, could not run for even a day.

In 2006 alone, the increased government revenues from petroleum and gas exploitation indicated that the shift toward nationalist state capitalism would provide a much-needed economic boost after the neoliberal policies of the past twenty years. The successful renegotiation with Argentina brought in an additional $110 million per month in 2006. The new royalties in the two largest fields were bringing in an additional $32 million per month.[13] In late October 2006, shortly before the government's six-month deadline for "migration" of the contracts was to expire, representatives of Petrobras, Repsol, and the other multinationals finally came to terms. Royalties of 82 percent for Bolivia and 18 percent for outside firms were locked in for coming decades, reversing the give-away deal cut with Sánchez de Lozada.

It is these improved terms and prospects, not an abstract idea of what radical nationalization *should* look like, that currently inform Bolivian perspectives. Even in its moderate form, this nationalization retains backing among the popular sectors that originally proposed it. The rollback of Sánchez de Lozada's "capitalization plan" should also bolster the government's hold over popular constituencies via the distribution of new revenues for social programs, if it sustains the rebuilding of YPFB, more favorable contracts, and transparent accounting.

Press coverage in the US and UK made it virtually impossible to understand what, in fact, had transpired, in part because the decree itself was branded a radical nationalist provocation with potentially destabilizing effects in the region.[14] Whereas the government partially fulfilled a demand supported in some fashion or other by all but a fraction of the population, media representations made it seem as though nationalization was evidence of Morales's authoritarian, anti-democratic tendencies—perhaps because George W. Bush bemoaned the "erosion of democracy in Bolivia" after the decree was announced. The *Financial Times* considered Morales, arguably the most democratic as well as the most popular of Bolivian presidents, "increasingly authoritarian," while the *Washington Post* decried the "nationalist fervor" allegedly sweeping Latin America, the implication being that the desire for sovereign control over natural resources was irrational.[15]

Unlike the precedents to which Morales referred in his speech on May Day, Decree 28701 did not expropriate foreign companies or prohibit them from operating in Bolivia, yet the press stated the opposite. The *Wall Street Journal*, for example, excoriated "Bolivia's decision to kick

out foreign energy companies," since refineries under Petrobras management "were going to be seized."[16] Implicit or explicit in much of the
coverage was the assumption that Bolivian developments were a direct
extension of the agenda of Hugo Chávez in Venezuela. In sum, across
the (admittedly narrow) ideological spectrum, press coverage in English
was ill-informed, misleading, and mistaken about particulars.

Agrarian Reform

Even more than nationalization of the mines, MNR hegemony stemmed
from the official sanction it gave to land takeovers in 1952–3. While
MAS's legitimacy is more likely to hinge on the fate of nationalization
of hydrocarbons, the government took a page from the MNR when it
announced its "agrarian revolution" on 16 May 2006. The move did not
respond to great pressure from below this time, but was based on recognition of the grossly uneven distribution of land in the country. Ninety
percent of small agricultural producers depend on 10 percent of the country's land for their livelihoods, while large and medium landholdings
account for 90 percent of all land—this is a staggering level of inequality,
even by Latin American standards.[17]

   The reform also suggests that the government is willing to use constitutional means to check the power of the most intransigent right-wing
opposition in the lowlands. This has antagonized the lowland elite, whose
formation after the 1950s hinged on the acquisition of *latifundia* (large
landed estates), often without legitimate right or title. Agribusiness development in the "half moon" crescent arc that passes from Pando, Beni,
and Santa Cruz through Tarija was also subsidized by the central government beginning in the mid-1950s under Siles and accelerating in the
1970s under General Banzer. Concentration of land was a notable feature
of neoliberal agrarian counter-reform in the 1980s and '90s, and today
as in the recent past, these lowland elites are the largest landholders in
Bolivia.

   More than nationalization—which stands to benefit all, albeit
unequally—it is the threat of agrarian reform in the lowlands that has
stoked the fires of reaction and increased pressures for regional autonomy.
Following the Brazilian example, there is evidence of landlords recruiting
paramilitary contingents to prevent takeovers of their land. Prefects elected

in December 2005 in the "half moon" territory are accountable to landed interests in their respective departments, dominated as a bloc by the elites and the Civic Committee of Santa Cruz. The strident voices denouncing MAS "authoritarianism" refer, above all, to the putative violation of their private property rights.

The thing to stress about the proposed agrarian reform, however, is that it is fully in keeping with constitutional principles. Despite its overblown rhetoric, like the nationalization decree, the agrarian reform declaration does not represent a radical point of departure for MAS. To begin with, it does not challenge the rights of private property legitimately acquired and titled. The reform is based, however, on one of the lasting progressive legacies of the 1938 constitution drafted by the national convention during the regime of Gen. Germán Busch. By constitutional law, the right to individual private property is not absolute. All property must fulfill a "social function," meaning that any lands not under productive cultivation may be confiscated by the state, with proper compensation. The sheer extent of land used for speculative rather than productive purposes, or simply lying abandoned, guarantees that even modest redistribution of land would benefit a large number of lowland peasant families. Here again, reform could strengthen MAS's appeal to, and hold over, popular movements, especially in rural areas which is where half the population still lives, while encroaching on the political domain of reactionary elites.

Constitutional Assembly

Alongside the nationalization of hydrocarbons, the other outstanding feature of the "October Agenda" was a demand for a constitutional assembly to "re-found" the nation. The assembly was thought to hold the key to breaking the monopoly on formal representation exercised by political parties. A new constitution, with a new system of local, regional, and national representation, would redesign relations between state and society in the direction of decolonization and democratization. Indigenous intellectuals and movements from the lowlands, and then popular and indigenous insurgents in Cochabamba and the highlands, were the first to articulate these demands. As the insurgent cycle that began in 2000 unfolded, the call became generalized. Trade unions, neighborhood organizations, street vendors' associations, colonizers' movements, and other groups sought to express themselves directly, to represent themselves without the mediation of professional politicians.

A handful of intellectuals crafted sophisticated proposals for the assembly, some of them envisioning creative new forms of ethnic and regional representation. Lively debate also took place in public forums, whether among autonomous grassroots groups or sponsored by state and non-governmental organizations. Nonetheless, there was no unifying proposal around which the different movements could rally, and for which they were willing to take to the streets. If electoral triumph highlighted the strength of the new national-popular bloc, lack of clear alternatives to the existing system of political representation illustrated a critical weakness.

If a new experiment with political representation was to be taken seriously, in keeping with the discourse of decolonization and social inclusion, then the election of delegates to the constitutional assembly would be the testing ground. Prior to the December 2005 elections, virtually all the parties in the campaign approved of a bloc of indigenous delegates to the assembly, especially since indigenous leadership had brought the assembly into being. When MAS unveiled its formula for the representation of delegates in March 2006, however, it rejected any form of collective representation according to ethnic criteria, trade union or neighborhood affiliation, or any of the other sorts of social association by which ordinary people organize their daily lives and express themselves politically (outside the occasional electoral context).

Representation would be based on existing electoral districts and on a one-person-one-vote principle. The only eligible candidates would be those who ran with a formal political party or citizens' group approved by the state. It appears that this utterly conventional liberal model of representation was a compromise that García Linera sought to bring the conservative lowland constituencies into a constitutional assembly that they looked on with great distrust. The formula also guaranteed the representation of political "minorities," meaning the weak traditional parties, since the highest vote-getter could only take two out of the three delegates in each district, regardless of how high a percentage the winner obtained. One delegate slot was automatically reserved for the runner-up.

In the end, the MAS went on to concede an additional bloc of regional delegates from each of the nine departments. This regional representation favored the demographically sparse "half-moon" where the conservative parties were based. Ironically, then, collective representation was allowed for the regions—a regionalist quota—to the benefit of the right. Yet it was denied for indigenous groups or for popular associations since this was seen as a non-liberal form of representation.

The other form of collective representation allowed, which passed without controversy, was gender-based. On every party's slate, women were to be one of the top two candidates for any delegate slot. In another apparent signal to the lowland right, García Linera declared in April that it was entirely possible that the assembly would modify no more than 10 to 20 percent of the existing constitution.[18]

In response to MAS's proposal, indigenous leaders met in Santa Cruz in February to demand a mixed system of representation. According to their own compromise model, 16 Indian delegates from the highlands and 16 from the lowlands were to be elected in community assemblies with gender parity for men and women, while the rest would be elected according to MAS's proposal of the principle of one citizen-one vote, with one third of all slots allotted to women and one third to younger men.

The indigenous proposal was quickly discounted, most vocally by García Linera, who argued that broadening representation beyond formal parties and civic groups could open the process up to hijacking by a right-wing movement determined to use the issue of regional autonomy to block the election of delegates and the instauration of the assembly. The argument was debatable, since Morales was at the high point of his popularity and the right was for the first time faced with substantial support for MAS within its own territory. Yet García Linera's argument could not be dismissed easily either: at stake was the fate of the upcoming referendum on regional autonomy, the interpretation and application of the July 2004 referendum on nationalization, and the "re-foundation" of the country.

A point that stands out in this *desencuentro*—the failed engagement between the MAS leadership and the social movements that sought to maintain their autonomy—is the tone the government adopted toward those to whom it had so recently looked for guidance and critical pressure on ceremonial occasions. MAS argued that indigenous groups no longer needed "special representation," since they had already achieved representation—through MAS. According to García Linera, those pressuring for direct collective representation demonstrated "a time-lag in their historical location. They continue in resistance, on the defensive in the face of the state, and it is hard for them to locate themselves in this new time of occupying structures of power."[19] Whatever their intent, such statements de-authorized, marginalized, and silenced indigenous demands. It was a new example of the condescension that has plagued Indian-left relations historically and that has pushed indigenous activists into more radically autonomous positions.

Where one might have expected resistance to this sort of administrative steamrolling, significant protest or mobilization was absent. Calls to organize an alternative popular assembly found no echo in what a leading Bolivian political theorist has called the "political subsoil."[20] Here again, at a decisive juncture, the social movements revealed a critical weakness. MAS would monopolize national-popular political representation in the assembly, acting as a centralizing force in relation to the movements that had brought it to power as well as regionalist opponents on the right. In effect, by blocking the presence of independent dissidents and movements in the assembly, MAS could bring the right into the process, as well as position itself as the new MNR—the new center of gravity in the revived political party system.[21]

This, then, was far more than a technical dispute. Though few acknowledged it at the time, the popular movements had lost a crucial battle. MAS had refused to open the constitutional assembly to the full spectrum of voices, to the wide array of social forces that had originally envisioned such a national debate and then made it possible through direct action. That refusal began the effective closure of the revolutionary process.

In the elections to the Constituent Assembly on 2 July 2006, MAS won 55 percent, or 137 of the 255 delegates. Though an unprecedented number were of popular class and ethnic extraction, they were not independent of, or autonomous from, MAS. Rather, they had been selected by the party and were directly accountable to it. MAS's numbers were double those of its nearest runner-up, former President Jorge Quiroga's PODEMOS, which had failed to make any headway since its bust in December 2005. Yet MAS still fell well short of the two-thirds threshold it had agreed to for approval of a new constitution. Nor was there any clear-cut path for MAS to bring other parties into a bloc that could achieve the two-thirds needed. Under the circumstances, it seemed that any constitution approved would be the product of significant compromise.

Despite the frustrating prospects ahead, the assembly inauguration in Sucre, on 6 August 2006, was a symbolically charged and historically unprecedented political festival. The last time national-popular forces had converged on Sucre had been in May and June of 2005. Tens of thousands of miners and Quechua-Aymara community peasants had arrived to prevent Hormando Vaca Diez, President of the Senate and representative of the regionalist right, from assuming executive power. This time it was to celebrate the constitutional assembly that popular actions since 2000 had made possible, though at the invitation of a government that had denied them direct representation in the assembly itself. Indian organizations from around the country, peasant and proletarian trade unions, and military corps with their marching bands processed together in disciplined formation for hour after hour. With their high spirits and proud regalia, they filled to overflowing Sucre's colonial-era plaza, which had been legally off-limits for Indian peasants until the mid-twentieth century.

No Bolivian political figure could have been more different from Vaca Diez than Silvia Lazarte, elected president of the constitutional assembly. An indigenous woman, she spoke Spanish like the citizens celebrating outside, as a second or third language. Like Evo Morales, she was raised in dire poverty and had become a veteran trade union leader for coca growers. Not least, as a peasant colonizer of lands in San Julián, Santa Cruz, she had confronted members of the lowland elite like Vaca Diez on their own turf.[22] Not until the 1960s had women been represented in any of Bolivia's previous twelve constitutional conventions. Never before had an indigenous person taken part. When she addressed the assembly, her high-pitched voice was passionate and intense, unlike the tones of any former occupant of her office, but very much like the other, anonymous feminine voices that had helped put her in such a place.

Openings and Closings

In many ways, Sucre reflected the changing times. There was now popular ethnic-class political representation, unlike anything witnessed before, in the executive, top ministries, congress, and the constitutional assembly. It would be virtually impossible to revert to past creole monopoly and outright indigenous exclusion. As we can see from looking at earlier moments, the present will have a lasting impact, not least in terms of political consciousness and how the majority of Bolivians interpret the past and project a desirable future. The overturning of the social order does indeed seem dramatic enough to call this a time of "*pachakuti.*"

If MAS itself is unable to meet the full aspirations of the popular majority, it did, at least initially, surpass the expectations many held for it. At the same time, MAS was never out to accomplish the most radical of goals. What marked MAS's initial policies was the effort to construct a national-popular bloc, with indigenous centrality but under party control, in order to carry out reforms from above. The goal is more or less explicit: integrate some of the cadre and leadership of the movements into the party-state nexus—without altering the monopoly political parties enjoy on formal political representation. It should come as no surprise that MAS put its organizational interests first in hopes of securing a stable basis on which to rule. Since 2002, electoral outcomes have defined the strategic space within which MAS moves.

The contemporary revolutionary process was initiated by insurgent rural and urban indigenous movements joined by other national-popular groups that eventually carried the MAS to power. In taking over the revolutionary process, the Morales-García Linera administration brought it to a provisional close. But it must also be said that the limitations shown by the revolutionary process in Bolivia are not only attributable to the limited horizons and intrinsic problems of the party.

There is the constraining international context on the one hand. On the other, the weaknesses of the popular movements themselves must lie at the heart of any convincing explanation. Not only were popular forces unable to sustain bottom-up pressures once MAS entered office; they could not persuade or coerce the new political leadership to accept alternative forms of political representation. Though the international press and punditry have tended to understand Morales in conjunction with Chávez as against Lula, Morales's agenda and the manner of its implementation are better thought of first in relation to the tense and shifting relations between the leadership and rank-and-file militants of the Bolivian movements that took center stage after 2000.

Conclusion

Quip Nayr Uñtasis Sartañani

The cycle of insurgency that began with the "Water War" in Cochabamba in 2000 acquired a revolutionary national dimension in the dramatic Indian and popular insurrection centered in El Alto in October 2003. That vast and spontaneous mobilization from below created a political opening that set the agenda for the reform of the hydrocarbons sector and for a constitutional assembly that was to rewrite the fundamental charter for the country. The strength and demands of social movements in the country swept away an atrophied neoliberal political order and swept into political office Evo Morales and his Movement to Socialism party in the December 2005 elections. In January 2006, Morales took over the governing palace, which no one claiming indigenous identity had ever occupied before.

MAS quickly responded to the October Agenda and received broad popular approval for its series of reform measures: "nationalization," "agrarian revolution," and convocation of the assembly. It thereby put the lowland right-wing forces on the defensive, and effectively defused the social movements that had initially issued the Morales government a timetable for fulfillment of their demands. The terms set for the constitutional assembly were especially significant for internal political realignments. Government concessions on representation in the assembly brought the right into a process it had bitterly opposed, and left the social movements with no representative other than MAS itself. By August 2006, after the inauguration of the assembly in Sucre, the MAS bid for hegemony in the country seemed to be remarkably successful. With the consolidation of power by MAS and the first steps towards political and economic reform under way, the revolutionary phase of "direct interference of the masses in historic events" seemed to draw to a close.

The historical process itself is by no means at an end, however, and new developments could conceivably move it in unsuspected directions. If MAS's hegemonic bid fails, right-wing resurgence and social mobilization may push the government in a more radical direction. If right-wing counter-revolutionary forces, abetted by the United States, recover from their historic setbacks, they could return to bring the process into a new stage of confrontation and crisis. If the social movements sense that right-wing elites are regaining the upper hand, their autonomous mobilization could reopen the process. But even if the revolutionary phase has come to an end, this period from 2000 to 2006 will leave powerful legacies for the history of the future.

The earlier revolutionary moments in the territory known today as "Bolivia" also had profound consequences, as we have seen throughout this book. The southern Andean indigenous insurgency of the early 1780s shaped the independence process and republican state-formation in the nineteenth century as well as elite and indigenous political memory until the present. The national revolution of the early 1950s likewise redefined economic and political relations in Bolivia for thirty years, until the neoliberal model sought to roll back its effects. The present conjuncture is also marked by a recollection and recovery of many of the features of the mid-twentieth century moment.

Complementary Opposites

The current historical transformation or *pachakuti* has brought about the collapse of the once triumphant neoliberal model instituted in the 1980s and mounted the greatest challenge yet seen to the historical structures of internal colonialism. The transformation has come about precisely through a convergence of the Indian tradition of struggle, most fully expressed in the 1770s to 1780s, and the national-popular struggle whose heyday was in the 1930s to early 1950s. The great revolution of 1780–1 was eventually put down by colonial counter-insurgency after creole allies repudiated Indian leadership and hegemony. 1952 was a middle-class- and creole-led revolution that succeeded in overturning the oligarchic liberal order thanks to the mobilization of working-class and Indian peasant forces. Today's revolutionary movement once again gained its strength from the encounter between the twin traditions of struggle and the dual sources of rural and urban, Indian and mestizo-creole, Andean communal and national-popular history. As in 1781, the political vision, initiative, and leadership in our own period have flowed first and foremost from indigenous forces. Yet, as in 1781, there remain tensions between the dual sources of power, and advances in the historical process will depend on the charged encounter—or *tinku*—between them.

In Andean culture, *tinku* means the coming together of two parts that are distinct and that may be in tension with one another, yet are also complementary and mutually constitutive. Lock and key must fit together for a box to open. Two travelers coming from different directions on the same road must encounter each other. Two tributary streams meet in a churning junction and merge to form a more powerful river. In northern Potosí towns, as was once widespread in the Andes, two halves of a community still face off in ritual combat on ceremonial occasions, and the release of energy in warrior combat provides a channeling of violence and fertilizing of natural, social, and sacred relations that is thought to benefit the community as a whole.[1] This Andean metaphor and practice of *tinku* provides a concept for thinking about the fraught, difficult, yet potentially fertile encounter and alliance between the Indian and national-popular traditions of struggle in Bolivia, past and present.

Though often at odds with one another or remote from one another historically, when these two traditions converge, as they have today, the frontiers between them blur. In September and early October 2003, rural Aymara communities initially spearheaded the defense of Bolivia's natural gas resources and national sovereignty in the face of private, transnational extraction. In mid-October 2003, as the city of El Alto became the critical point of confrontation between neoliberal state power and radical popular forces, insurgent mobilization drew from two traditions of collective organization and political militancy. Courageous protests in western neighborhoods such as Villa Ingenio—formed by Aymara migrants from the countryside—and in southern neighborhoods such as Santiago II—with a significant presence of former mine workers relocated after the neoliberal structural adjustment of 1985—fed into each other, and combined with powerful effects.

The political ascent, ideology, and leadership of the MAS government also reflect this convergence. MAS finally came to power only after long conflicts, which debilitated popular and left projects, were partly superseded through collective grassroots mobilization. First, tensions over the self-appointment of proletarian and left organizations to provide political direction for peasant forces have been present for much of the twentieth century, reflecting differing class and ethnic political agendas. During the 1990s, even after the proletarian leadership of the COB had waned, conflicts persisted between peasant trade union groups and autonomous Indian intellectuals. When Felipe Quispe brought a radical *indianista* program to the CSUTCB after 1998, his highland Aymara forces still remained at loggerheads with the *cocalero* movement headed by Morales in Cochabamba. *Cocalero* trade-unionists, anchored in anti-imperialist class identities, did not share the same ethnic discourse and saw the Indianist agenda as divisive.

Yet the ground was shifting in the new millennium. Indigenous cultural affirmation had been growing in the 1990s, in both the Andean highlands and Amazonian lowlands. Aymara, Quechua, Guaraní, Moxeño, and other lowland indigenous identities were no longer claimed exclusively by a radical intellectual minority or relatively marginal political representatives. Nor was ethnic discourse confined to under-funded state agencies, non-governmental organizations, or academics hoping to defuse social conflict through an imported, upbeat multiculturalism. The traditional political elite responded scornfully and dismissively to highland Indian insurgency beginning in 2000, yet the strength of indigenous mobilization reinforced cultural affirmation in society at large. As Evo Morales staked out his electoral strategy for the MAS, and pursued it with increasing success, he and his party acquired an ever more—not less—indigenous profile. In the eyes of international and domestic media, in the eyes of the populace, and in his own eyes, the leftist trade union comrade was now also an Indian brother. "*El compañero Evo*" had also become "*el hermano Evo*," reflecting his place in national-popular and indigenous communal parlance.

The convergence of the dual traditions of struggle, and the primacy of the indigenous element, was further symbolized by the alliance of Evo Morales with Alvaro García Linera in the 2005 elections. Since the consolidation of MAS in the mid-1990s, this "political vehicle" included not only *cocalero* representatives but creole leftists from earlier generations of struggle, such as the one-time Trotskyist mine worker and trade-unionist Filemón Escobar whose political roots go back to the 1950s, or Antonio and Osvaldo "Chato" Peredo Leigue, who were part of the *guevarista* guerrilla movements of the 1960s and early 1970s. García Linera was also of the creole Marxist left, yet his political and intellectual trajectory led him to engage directly with Indian radicalism. He participated

alongside Felipe Quispe in the Tupac Katari Guerrilla Army in the early
1990s and, after his arrest, as a theorist of social movements, he supported
Indian struggles in the present. Both Morales and García Linera were in
fact of more complex political backgrounds than either category—Indian
or national-popular—would suggest. Yet in the 2005 campaign, their
personae as running mates were that of the Indian president and his
middle-class creole leftist *aide-de-camp*.

Judging from history, the encounter between Indian and left/popular
nationalist elements is likely to be touchy and transitory. It remains to be
seen how the Morales-García Linera duo will hold up, and how the MAS
will evolve as a party in relation to other indigenous forces and indigenous
demands in the country. The MAS government came to power urging
decolonization of the state and of Bolivian politics and society. Yet its
commitment to actual policies and institutional changes that would bring
out lasting decolonization may well erode as it pursues its nationalist reform
agenda and seeks legitimacy among the middle classes. The first such sign
was the government's refusal to introduce changes in the system of political
representation for the constituent assembly. Vice-President García Linera's
own position was that the constituent assembly was no longer so necessary
with the MAS now in power, and that the indigenous majority had de
facto representation through MAS, in the executive and legislative branches
of the state and in the assembly. The argument was that the very power
of MAS was proof of effective decolonization.

The current political ascendancy of the MAS is indeed significant and
remarkable. Yet MAS's argument is problematic because of the way in
which it converts the interests of the party into the interests of the indigenous majority. If MAS is displaced politically, as will occur sooner or
later, there would be no lasting structures or institutions to secure ongoing
indigenous political representation. Furthermore, if MAS confides too
much in itself and its momentary strength, ignoring indigenous forces
that adopt a position autonomous from the state, or expresses criticism
of the ruling party, it will run a grave risk. If a new phase of crisis opens
up, it would stand to lose the convergent bases of support that brought
it to power in the first place.

Meanwhile, those Indian and grassroots political voices and movements
that assert autonomy from the state will also confront difficulties of their
own. Renewed radicalism in the present juncture, while MAS stands out as

the only viable national alternative to the traditional political order, runs the risk of isolation and irrelevance. In a future moment of crisis, radical mobilization that undermines MAS risks opening the door for a right-wing return to power. This is not an abstract possibility, but one that occurred during the UDP debacle and neoliberal triumph of the early to mid-1980s.

Memories of the Future

Before the events of October 2003, no one anticipated the startling transformations that awaited the country. While the neoliberal model was evidently in decline after 1997, and entering crisis after 2000, there was no new alternative project for political and economic reorganization on the domestic or international horizon. The viability of a socialist or a nationalist political economy seemed to have little backing in professional or technical circles. Yet even if a swing of the pendulum back towards a national project—reacting against the pro-imperial policies under neoliberalism —might have been imagined as a possible development, there was no sense of what the nationalism of the early twenty-first century might turn out to be. Least of all was there an expectation of a new national-popular formation with Indian centrality, the feature which distinguishes Bolivia in the general context of Latin America today.

The future is unforeseeable, as ever, yet one certainty is that the current revolutionary moment will leave legacies and provide lessons for future generations. This idea is captured by the Aymara phrase that heads this section: "To walk ahead while looking back" (*quip nayr uñtasis sartañani*). Aymara historians have taken up this expression to orient current cultural and political action according to the memory of earlier struggles waged by their ancestors. For example, the Andean Oral History Workshop (THOA) dedicated years of archival and oral history work to recovering the nearly forgotten experience of Santos Marka T'ula and the *caciques-apoderados* who fought for community rights to land, education, and citizenship in the first half of the twentieth century. This salvaged memory helped galvanize efforts to reconstitute older *ayllu* territories and traditional systems of political authority within Indian communities in the 1990s.[2] We can expect that the struggles and achievements of the social movements since 2000 will likewise orient the vision and fortify the aspirations of radical forces for decades to come. The rapid advances and accumulated power of Indian and popular movements has raised bright hopes that will remain as expectations for a redemptive future.

Yet recent history will leave its share of darker memories as well. The deepening crisis of Bolivian society since the late 1990s reached its nadir in October 2003. If the Days of October stand out as a high point for the rising tide of popular resistance and demands, the events of the time will also be remembered, especially in the crucible city of El Alto, as Black October. In the aftermath of vicious state repression, Bolivians around the country hung the national tricolor flag from their homes with an added black bow of mourning for those who died.

With this in mind, it is worth summoning up another, more devastating image of looking backward while moving into the future. The German Jewish Marxist critic Walter Benjamin, writing as winds of war and genocide were blowing about him in 1940, expressed a tragic account of the historical consciousness of catastrophe:

> A Klee painting named "Angelus Novus" shows an angel looking as though he is about to move away from something he is fixedly contemplating. His eyes are staring, his mouth is open, his wings are spread. This is how one pictures the angel of history. His face is turned toward the past. Where we perceive a chain of events, he sees one single catastrophe which keeps piling wreckage upon wreckage and hurls it in front of his feet. The angel would like to stay, awaken the dead, and make whole what has been smashed. But a storm is blowing from Paradise; it has got caught in his wings with such violence that the angel can no longer close them. The storm irresistibly propels him into the future to which his back is turned, while the pile of debris before him grows skyward. This storm is what we call progress.

The Aymara historians' usage of *quip nayr uñtasis sartañani* often carries with it a sense of salvaging the past for the sake of justice and redemption. This is reminiscent of the task Benjamin set for emancipatory history:

> To articulate the past historically does not mean to recognize it "the way it really was" (Ranke). It means to seize hold of a memory as it flashes up at a moment of danger. Historical materialism wishes to retain that image of the past which unexpectedly appears to man singled out

by history at a moment of danger. The danger affects both the content of the tradition and its receivers ... Only that historian will have the gift of fanning the spark of hope in the past who is firmly convinced that *even the dead* will not be safe from the enemy if he wins.[3]

Yet it is also important to allow the tragic vision of Benjamin's Angel of History within the notion of *quip nayr uñtasis sartañani*. The tradition of Indian struggle that this book has highlighted can only be understood in relation to the dark and enduring historical problem of internal colonialism in Bolivia. The recent violence waged by the state against Aymaras in El Alto and against Quechua and Aymara peasants in the countryside will also remain in the political consciousness of Indian activists, leaders, and community institutions, as well as in the minds of men and women in ordinary walks of life.

Zulema Flores recalled being on the streets in the El Alto district of Santiago II, a stronghold of resettled miners, on 10 October 2003:

> The sky clouded over. Night, with its immense black cloak, began to cover the city. Who would have thought that that night so much blood would flow, especially in Santiago II where I live. I went out at one point from my room and headed to the Plaza of the Miner. When I heard shots of tear gas being fired, we all ran for refuge. Over the next hours, the sounds were different, shots of rubber bullets and even machine-gun blasts. The fear I had been trying to hide then increased and I started to cry. That night I couldn't find a way to sleep. The sound of the shots was more frequent, and a helicopter flew overhead again and again, causing incredible panic. That night and the following ones were an unending nightmare that will remain in my mind until the last day of my existence.[4]

Jhaneth Callisaya described her family's experience in the heavily Aymara district of Villa Esperanza in El Alto on 12 October 2003:

> Black, dark ... I don't know how to describe that Sunday afternoon that was the most horrible I have ever lived through ... Around two o'clock there was a bloody attack against the neighbors on the principal avenue and in the vicinity of my neighborhood. My mother

arrived at the house around four in the afternoon. She told us that armed soldiers arrived and were firing with bullets and rubber bullets at the neighbors, and that there were already two dead. Then she went out again ... When my mother returned at six o'clock, she said: "Go into your rooms." "Why?" we asked. She explained that behind our house the soldiers were shooting at anyone walking around, and that we could be hit by stray bullets. We were all more scared than ever as we continued to hear the shots, and there were a lot of them; it seemed that they would never stop ... I wish all this had been a dream and not reality. My whole family was safe; but with a memory we will never forget. One day we will recount the experience to our children.[5]

For others, however, what would remain was example and inspiration. One resident of La Paz, Iván Salazar, recalled the experience of solidarity during the Days of October:

I had the opportunity to engage with the others who make up our city, people who until then seemed unremarkable to me. I'm thinking, for example, of my neighbor Lucho, a man in his forties who showed solidarity with the marching miners by offering a little relief with a glass of water, and who spoke to me about the era of the UDP, perhaps with a little nostalgia ... I was particularly struck by Doña Elvira, an elderly woman who spent her whole life cooking in the homes of rich people. This lady, probably making a superhuman effort, collected all the vegetables and noodles she could, and used them to fix a soup that she distributed to the people wandering in the streets. Some were marchers who'd arrived from the interior; others were simply poor people from the neighborhood. These two examples speak to me of the enormous solidarity the *paceños* have, perhaps because we have lived through times like this before ...

At the time, his experience prompted a deep shift in individual subjectivity as well as collective awareness:

I am not the same person after these events. I changed my way of thinking and feeling about democracy and this city. Definitely, my life is now oriented toward the future—to appreciate my freedom and my strength to bring about changes that lead toward common welfare.[6]

Freddy Limachi, a resident of El Alto, reminisced about the darkness:

Fear, anger, despair, and other sentiments overcame Bolivians in "Black" October. Chaos, instability, and abnormality reigned in the streets of El Alto and La Paz.

Yet there were also images of light for him:

Demands for democracy and the defense of [national] property wrote an important page in the history of Bolivia and in the heart and memory of every Bolivian: for some because of the loss of a loved one, for others because of the hunger or impossibility of walking peacefully in the street, but above all because from now on everyone will have in his memory that glorious scene of men and women fighting for their rights and future, an event that they will recount to their descendants and that will allow democracy to be built . . .

There was such a feeling of patriotism that came over us that many of us started singing "Long live my patria Bolivia" with all our hearts and souls in a loud voice or in our breasts with that feeling that in the moment spread to even the least involved. There was such happiness that on one of the loudspeakers someone said, "*Vecinonaca: Niau uca gringoja historiar pasjhe, ma cobardempacha aca diajata mistshua; Alajpacharu y Tatitujar yuspagarta aka jach'a victoriata. Takhenaca bolivianophjtaw, ucata janiu ch'ecaznna saphjamti sapsmahua. Yuspagaraps'jmawa.*" ["Neighbors: The gringo (Sánchez de Lozada) is already history, one more coward who is gone from our days. I give thanks to our dear Father and the Upper World for granting us this great victory. You are all Bolivians. Therefore I say to you: do not to be divided or indifferent. Thank you."]

These events were transcendental for our lives . . . As a friend of mine said, this is the beginning of the renovation of the country and our lives.[7]

Carmen Sandoval Jordán, a resident of Villa Adela in El Alto, drew lessons for future organizing:

> October was a very important step forward because that's when we saw that when we are unified, not always following the leaders, we can do things. On our own, the people—we who go through the greatest difficulties in life, who have no work, who only have 5 *bolivianos* a day to give something to our families—we are the ones who went out and stood up . . . I have learned from October, learned a lot . . . I'm really from El Alto, but of miner origin, and that struggle stays with you . . . I believe the struggle of October is going to return, and we have to be ready.[8]

The full importance of this historic moment goes well beyond Evo Morales and the fortunes of the MAS as a pretender to hegemonic state power. The experience of organizing, and the memory of popular power in a revolutionary process has been engraved in individual consciousness and will remain as a resource in popular urban neighborhoods and rural communities, in collective mobilizations for generations to come. Its effects will be felt in ongoing pressures for indigenous political participation, territory, and self-government. It will fortify youth, women, intellectuals, activists, and professionals in their aspirations for social justice and equality. Its reverberations will stir cultural and spiritual visions of *pachakuti* in our time.

These are consequences of the present whose force will be difficult to obstruct or reverse in the near future. And yet, if history has shown that revolutionary moments leave an indelible mark on the future, it has shown that internal colonial and class hierarchies are durable structures as well. Both revolution and internal colonialism will remain in sharp outline as people in the land called Bolivia walk forward into the early twenty-first century.

Notes

Chapter 1

1 Tom Lewis and Oscar Olivera, eds, *¡Cochabamba! Water War in Bolivia* (Boston, 2004), pp. 37–8.

2 Departments, of which Bolivia has nine, are the principal administrative divisions of the country, and are run by prefects. Departments are further divided into provinces, of which sub-prefects are in charge. Eighty-six percent of total gas reserves are in the department of Tarija and 11 percent in Santa Cruz.

3 For a regional Andean perspective, see Paul W. Drake and Eric Hershberg, eds, *State and Society in Conflict: Comparative Perspectives on Andean Crises* (Pittsburgh, PA, 2006).

4 Racial and ethnic categories are as slippery in Bolivia as anywhere else in Latin America, despite the greater polarization since colonial times between those who are defined, and define themselves, as "Indians" and those who are not. Our terminology follows common usage, though such usage is constantly being redefined. "Aymara" and "Quechua," ethnic terms deriving from twentieth-century linguistic anthropology rather than earlier historical self-attribution, have gained currency in recent decades. Not all "laborers of Aymara descent" would consider themselves "Aymara" or "Indian," especially given the stigma attached to the terms historically. Yet political conflicts have contributed to processes of ethnic identification since the 1990s. We use "indigenous" and "Indian" interchangeably. "Mestizo" implies a racial or cultural mixture of Indian and European ancestry, yet in the highlands it carries a marked sense of difference from "Indians" or popular sectors of "Aymara descent" (also referred to as "cholos"). In valley regions like Cochabamba, "mestizo" is more frequently applied to the peasantry and urban popular sectors. "Creole" refers to people thought to be of predominantly European ancestry who are raised (from the Spanish *criar*) in the Americas.

5 We work with René Zavaleta Mercado's notion of the "national-popular," a term that first appeared sketchily in Italian theorist Antonio Gramsci's prison notebooks. The insurrectionary "multitude" (or "masses") that struggled to realize "national-popular" projects, according to Zavaleta, was formed through a process of political articulation among classes that tended to be fragmented in relation to each other: the proletariat, progressive fractions of the middle class, and the peasantry. In the latter half of the twentieth century, this articulation entailed proletarian centrality. Zavaleta also explored the national content of popular projects earlier in Bolivian history. He understood the "democratic" aspect of these projects as the self-determination of civil society, or of the "multitude" as its agent in moments of struggle. See René Zavaleta Mercado, *Las masas en noviembre* (La Paz, 1983) and *Lo nacional-popular en Bolivia* (Mexico, 1986); as well as Luis Tapia's major

study of Zavaleta, *La producción del conocimiento local* (La Paz, 2002). See also, "Introduction to Zavaleta," *New Left Review* 73 (May–June 1971), pp. 58–62.

6 Despite the impressive history of trade-unionism in the country, the term "working class" must be used advisedly in light of the decomposition of organized labor, and its "informalization" since 1985, when neoliberal structural adjustment went into effect. If a process of "reproletarianization" can be said to be underway in areas such as El Alto, this can only refer to small-scale, family-run, artisanal manufacturing and service activities. thirty-five percent of alteños describe themselves as "workers." Yet the once proud mine-working population shrank dramatically after the closure of state-run tin mines in 1985, and labors today under extremely precarious conditions. The COB (the Bolivian Workers' Central) languished as a political force during the 1990s after rejecting peasant proposals to adjust the proportions of peasant and proletarian representation in the national leadership.

7 See the historical and contemporary analyses in Forrest Hylton, Felix Patzi, Sergio Serulnikov and Sinclair Thomson, *Ya es otro tiempo el presente: Cuatro momentos de insurgencia indígena* (La Paz, 2003), as well as the prefatory essay by Adolfo Gilly. Our introduction posits the long-term formation of an indigenous political culture of insurrection in the Bolivian Andes, one which has shaped current patterns of resistance in urban and trade union spheres as well as the countryside.

8 Hugo José Suárez, *Una semana fundamental: 10–18 de Octubre* (La Paz, 2003), pp. 41–51; Luis Gómez, *El Alto de pie: Una insurrección aymara en Bolivia* (La Paz, 2004).

9 In all three countries, overlap between mother tongue and ethnic self-identification is closer in the countryside than in the cities. The distance has increased with the growth of shanty towns, which proliferated under, but pre-date, the neoliberal period. See Mike Davis, *Planet of Slums* (New York, 2006), pp. 50–63; Xavier Albó, "Cuoteo étnico: ¿Sí o no?," *Pulso* No. 276, December 2004; Rafael Loayza, "La construcción de una identidad excluida," *Barataria* 1:1 (2004), p. 40; Seminario de las Naciones Unidas (UN) Sobre la Recopilación y Desglose de Datos Relativos a los Pueblos Indígenas, New York, 19–24 January, 2004: www.un.org

10 The concept of internal colonialism which circulated in Latin America in the 1970s and 1980s has retained special force and developed in original ways in the Bolivian context. See Silvia Rivera Cusicanqui, "La raíz: Colonizadores y colonizados," in Xavier Albó y Raul Barrios, eds, *Violencias encubiertas en Bolivia* (La Paz, 1993), pp. 33–5; and Seemin Qayum, "Creole Imaginings: Race, Space, and the Making of Republican Bolivia," Ph.D. Thesis, Goldsmiths College, University of London (2002), pp. 25–9. On the Latin American context, see Peter Wade, *Blackness and Race Mixture in Colombia* (Baltimore, MD, 1993), pp. 147–8; idem, *Race and Ethnicity in Latin America* (London, 1997), pp. 64–7.

11 For the full text of the speech, see Pablo Stefanoni and Hervé do Alto, *Evo Morales: De la coca al palacio* (La Paz, 2006), pp. 157–61.

12 See our introduction to Hylton et al., *Ya es otro tiempo el presente*, pp. 5–17.

13 Benito Juárez, Mexican president from 1858–64, and again from 1866–72, can be seen as the first. An orphan from a Zapotec-speaking peasant family, Juárez achieved heroic stature as a leader in his country's liberal Reform process and in the resistance to French imperial intervention in Mexico. Alejandro Toledo, whose mediocre term in Peru lasted from 2001 to 2006, was born in a poor Ancash highland village and migrated to the coastal industrial city of Chimbote when he was a boy. Toledo invoked indigenous Andean motifs at his own inauguration, yet he tended to be seen in Peruvian public opinion less as an "Indian" than an acculturated "cholo," and his presidency was not associated with any indigenous political movement.

14 For the full text, see Stefanoni and do Alto, *Evo Morales*, pp. 130–56.

15 For an incisive survey of representations in the foreign and domestic media, see James Dunkerley, "Evo Morales, the 'Two Bolivias', and the Third Bolivian Revolution," *Journal of Latin American Studies* 39 (January 2007), pp. 133–67.

Chapter 2

1 See Adolfo Gilly, "Bolivia, una revolución del siglo XXI," *Perfil de La Jornada* (México, D.F.), 2 March 2004: www.jornada.unam.mx

2 For Marx and Engels, capitalist industrialization creates the very working class that will inevitably overthrow it: "What the bourgeoisie, therefore, produces, above all, is its own grave-diggers." See "Manifesto of the Communist Party" [1848], in Robert C. Tucker, ed., *The Marx-Engels Reader*, 2nd ed. (New York, 1978), p. 483.

3 Sinclair Thomson, *We Alone Will Rule: Native Andean Politics in the Age of Insurgency* (Madison WI, 2002).

4 Idem, "Revolutionary Memory in Bolivia: Anticolonial and National Projects from 1781 to 1952," in Merilee Grindle and Pilar Domingo, eds, *Proclaiming Revolution: Bolivia in Comparative Perspective* (Cambridge, MA and London, 2003), pp. 117–34.

5 Gilly's article has been translated into English as "Bolivia: The First Twenty-First-Century Revolution," *Socialism and Democracy* 19:3 (September 2005), pp. 41–54. See also Raúl Zibechi's contribution to the same volume, "Subterranean Echoes: Resistance and Politics 'desde el sótano'," pp. 13–39, which examines Bolivia in comparative perspective.

6 For an early assertion that the events of October constituted a "rebellion" but not a "revolution," see the interview with political scientist Fernando Mayorga in *Juguete Rabioso*, 26 October 2003.

7 Leon Trotsky, *History of the Russian Revolution* (New York, 1999 [1932]), p. 17.

8 Hylton and Thomson, *Ya es otra tiempo el presente*, pp. 5–17.

9 Although in fact there are significant differences among them, examples of the stimulating recent work include Pablo Mamani, Felix Patzi, Silvia Rivera, Luis Tapia, Alvaro García Linera, Raúl Prada, and Raquel Gutiérrez, Adolfo Gilly, and Raúl Zibechi. The name of the Comuna group formed by García Linera, Gutiérrez, Prada and Tapia refers not only to the traditional Andean community but to the spontaneously organized, popular-democratic government of the 1871 Paris Commune. For Comuna, see *El fantasma insomne: Pensando el presente desde el Manifiesto Comunista* (La Paz, 1999); *El regreso de la Bolivia plebeya* (La Paz, 2000); *Tiempos de rebelión* (La Paz, 2001); *Pluriverso: Teoría política boliviana* (La Paz, 2001); *Democratizaciones plebeyas* (La Paz, 2002); *Memorias de octubre* (La Paz, 2004); *Horizontes y límites del Estado y el poder* (La Paz, 2005).

10 For more on indigenous re-territorialization and grassroots autonomy, see Pablo Mamani, *El rugir de la multitudes: La fuerza de los levantamientos indígenas en Bolivia/Qollasuyu* (La Paz, 2004); Alvaro García Linera, "State Crisis, Popular Power," *New Left Review* 37 (January–February 2006), pp. 73–86; Zibechi, "Subterranean Echoes: Resistance and Politics 'desde el sótano.'"

11 Gonzalo Chávez, quoted in "Bolivian Nods to Indian Roots," *Washington Post*, 22 January 2006. See also, Carlos Toranzo, *Rostros de la democracia* (La Paz, 2005), p. 15.

12 Thomson, *We Alone Will Rule*.

13 On the colonial and contemporary Andean semantics of the term, see Thérèse Bouysse-Cassagne and Olivia Harris, "Pacha: En torno al pensamiento aymara," in Bouysse-Cassagne et al., *Tres reflexiones sobre el pensamiento aymara*, pp. 31–5.

14 Karl Marx, "The Eighteenth Brumaire of Louis Bonaparte" [1852], in Tucker, ed., *The Marx-Engels Reader*, pp. 595–7.

15 Idem, "Letter to the Editorial Board of *Otechestvennye Zapiski*," in Teodor Shanin, ed., *Late Marx and the Russian Road: Marx and the Peripheries of Capitalism* (New York, 1983), p. 136.

Chapter 3

1 Godoy's memoirs are cited in Boleslao Lewin, *La rebelión de Túpac Amaru y los orígenes de la independencia de hispanoamérica* (1st ed., 1943; expanded 3rd ed., Buenos Aires, 1967), p. 413.

2 On Bourbon reform and rebellion in the Andes, see Scarlett O'Phelan Godoy, *Rebellions and Revolts in Eighteenth-Century Peru and Upper Peru* (Cologne, 1985); Brooke Larson, *Cochabamba, 1550–1900: Colonialism and Agrarian Transformation in Bolivia* (Durham, NC, 1998 [1st ed. 1988]); John Fisher, Allan Kuethe and Anthony McFarlane, eds, *Reform and Insurrection in Bourbon New Granada and Peru* (Baton Rouge, LA, 1990); and Sergio Serulnikov, *Subverting Colonial Authority: Challenges to Spanish Rule in Eighteenth-Century Southern Andes* (Durham, NC, 2003).

3 Alfredo Moreno Cebrián, *El corregidor de indios y la economía peruana en el siglo XVIII (los repartos forzosos de mercancías)* (Madrid, 1977); Jurgen Golte, *Repartos y rebeliones: Túpac Amaru y las contradicciones de la economía colonial* (Lima, 1980).

4 Serulnikov, *Subverting Colonial Authority*.

5 Sinclair Thomson, *We Alone Will Rule*. On the modes, methods, and dynamics of insurrectionary political culture historically, see Hylton and Thomson, "Introducción," in Hylton et al., pp. 5–17.

6 Cited in Lewin, *La rebelión*, pp. 119–20. The conspiracy was discovered before it could be put into effect, yet the manifesto issued by the group anticipated pronouncements and programs later in the century, including that of Tupaj Amaru.

7 Thomson, *We Alone Will Rule*.

8 See Lewin, *La rebelión*; O'Phelan, *Rebellions*; Fernando Cajías, *Oruro 1781: Sublevación de indios y rebelión criolla* (La Paz, 2004), 2 vols; Thomson, *We Alone Will Rule*; Serulnikov, *Subverting*.

9 Archivo General de Indias (AGI) Buenos Aires 319, "Cuaderno No. 4," pp. 60v, 77.

10 Javier Mendoza, *La mesa coja: Historia de la Proclama de la Junta Tuitiva del 16 de julio de 1809* (La Paz, 1997).

11 René Arze Aguirre, *La participación popular en la independencia de Bolivia* (La Paz, 1987).

12 John Lynch, *The Spanish American Revolutions, 1808–1826* (2nd ed., New York, 1986). Arze Aguirre, *La participación popular*. Brian Hamnett, "Process and Pattern: A Re-examination of the Ibero-American Independence Movements, 1808–1926," *Journal of Latin American Studies*. 29:2 (May 1997), pp. 279–328.

13 "Domination without hegemony" is contrasted with Antonio Gramsci's notion of a "hegemonic" social formation in which the dominant group rules over subalterns not only through coercion but with a substantial degree of legitimacy achieved through moral and intellectual leadership. See Ranajit Guha, *Dominance without Hegemony: History and Power in Colonial India* (Cambridge, MA, 1997), pp. xii–xiii, 20–3. On hegemony in Bolivia, see René Zavaleta Mercado, *Lo nacional-popular en Bolivia* (Mexico, 1986), pp. 132–9; on its absence in the Andean republics of the nineteenth century, and especially Bolivia, see Brooke Larson, *Trials of Nation-Making: Liberalism, Race, and Ethnicity in the Andes, 1810–1910* (Cambridge, 2004), pp. 8–15. See also, Antonio Gramsci, *Selections from the Prison Notebooks* (New York, 1971), pp. 50–60; Perry Anderson, "The Antinomies of Antonio Gramsci," *New Left Review* 100 (November–December 1976), pp. 5–78; Raymond Williams, *Marxism and Literature* (London, 1977), pp. 112–16.

Chapter 4

1 Tristan Platt, "Liberalism and Ethnocide in the Southern Andes," *History Workshop Journal* 17 (1984), pp. 3–16.

2 Cited in John Lynch, *The Spanish American Revolutions, 1808–1826,* (2nd ed., New York, 1986), p. 285.

3 For a splendid synthetic and comparative analysis of Indian-state relations in the nine-teenth-century Andes, see Brooke Larson, *Trials of Nation-Making: Liberalism, Race, and Ethnicity in the Andes 1810–1910* (Cambridge, 2004).

4 Rossana Barragán, "El Estado pactante: Gobiernos y pueblos: La configuración estatal y sus fronteras en Bolivia, 1825–80" unpublished doctoral thesis, Ecole des Hautes Etudes en Sciences Sociales (France), 2002, 2 volumes.

5 Erick Langer, "Espacios coloniales y economías nacionales: Bolivia y el norte argentino (1810–1930)," *Historia y Cultura* 17 (1990), pp. 69–94.

6 On mid-century demographics, see José María Dalence, *Bosquejo estadístico de Bolivia, 1846* (La Paz, 1975). Brooke Larson's *Cochabamba, 1550–1900: Colonialism and Agrarian Transformation in Bolivia* (1988; 2nd ed., Durham, NC, 1998) elucidates the political economy of this key region and where it fits in the broader southern Andean economic space over the long colonial period. Erick Langer's forthcoming research on southern Bolivia and transnational peasant markets in the 1840s and '50s should clarify the republican picture considerably.

7 For Bolivia, and the Atlantic world, in the mid-nineteenth century, see James Dunkerley, *Americana: The Americas in the World around 1850* (London, 2000).

8 Pilar Mendieta Parada, "De Tupac Katari a Zárate Willka: Alianzas, pactos, resistencia y rebelión en Mohoza" (La Paz, 2000), pp. 5–6. Marta Irurozqui, "El bautismo de la violencia: Indígenas patriotas en la revolución de 1870 en Bolivia," *Historia y Cultura* 28–9 (2003), pp. 149–78; Forrest Hylton, "Tierra común: Caciques, artesanos e intelectuales radicales y la rebelión de Chayanta," in Hylton et al., *Ya es otro tiempo el presente,* p. 139. Idem, "El federalismo insurgente: Una aproximación a Juan Lero, los comunarios y la Guerra Federal," *Tinkazos: Revista de las ciencias sociales bolivianas* 16 (2004), p. 116.

9 Erick Langer, "El liberalismo y la abolición de la comunidad indígena en el siglo XIX," *Historia y Cultura* 16 (1988), pp. 50–95.

10 Tristan Platt, *Estado boliviano y ayllu andino: Tierra y tributo en el norte de Potosí* (Lima, 1983), pp. 73–111. Erwin P. Greishaber, "Resistencia indígena a la venta de tierras comunales en el departamento de La Paz, 1881–1920," *Data* 1 (1991), pp. 113–44.

11 Leaders were known as *caciques* (Oruro, Potosí) or *apoderados* (La Paz, Cochabamba, Sucre). See the path-breaking work of Silvia Rivera Cusicanqui, *"Oprimidos pero no vencidos": Luchas del campesinado aymara-quechwa, 1900–80,* 4th ed. (La Paz, 2003 [1983]); Taller de Historia Oral Andina (THOA), *Santos Marka T'ula, el cacique apoderado de las comunidades de Qallapa* (La Paz, 1988); Carlos B. Mamani Condori, *Taraqu: Masacre, guerra y "Renovación" en la biografía de Eduardo L. Nina Quispe, 1866–1935* (La Paz, 1991); Esteban Alejo Ticona and Leandro Condori Chura, *El escribano de los caciques apoderados/Kasikinakan purirarkunakan quillqiripa* (La Paz, 1993); Juan Félix Árias (Waskar Ari Chachaki), *Historia de una esperanza: Los apoder-ados espiritualistas de Chuquisaca, 1936–1964* (La Paz, 1994); Roberto Choque Canqui and Esteban Ticona Alejo, *Sublevación y masacre de 1921: Jesús de Machaqa* (La Paz, 1996); Marcelo Fernández, "El poder de la palabra: Documento y memoria oral en la resistencia de Waqimarka contra la expansión latifundista (1874–1930)," thesis in Sociology, Universidad Mayor de San Andrés, 1996.

12 Marie-Danielle Demélas, "Sobre jefes legítimos y 'vagos' ", *Historia y Cultura* 8 (1985), pp. 51–73. Árias, *Historia de una esperanza,* pp. 28–9; Pilar Mendieta

Mendoza, "El movimiento de los apoderados, 1880–1899," in *De la reciprocidad a la rebelión: Estado y propiedad de la tierra en el siglo XIX*, Fascículo 4, in *La Razón* (1999), p. 12. See also Mendieta's forthcoming dissertation from the Universidad de San Marcos (Lima).

13 Marta Irurozqui, *Elites en litigio: La venta de tierras de comunidad en Bolivia, 1880–1899* (Lima, 1993).

14 Quoted in Carlos Mamani, *Taraqu*, p. 57.

15 Pilar Mendieta, "Entre el caudillismo y la modernidad: Poder local y política en la provincia de Inquisivi: El caso de Mohoza (1880–1889)," Tesis de Maestría, CESU-CEBEM, 2000, pp. 122–30.

16 José Luis Roca, "Oruro y la Revolución Federal," *Historia y Cultura* 6 (1983), pp. 113–31.

17 "Carta de José Manuel Pando a Severo Fernández Alonso, Caracollo, 3 de marzo, 1899," *Boletín Oficial No. 56*, La Paz, 8 de marzo de 1899, p. 2.

18 For Chaparro's testimony, see Corte Suprema de Justicia, Oruro (CSJ), *Juan Lero y Proceso Peñas*, vol. 3, fol. 500. On Andean peasant historical consciousness, see our introduction to *Ya es otro tiempo el presente*, pp. 5–17.

19 Ibid., vol. 2, fol. 353.

20 Ibid., vol. 6, fol. 1078.

21 Ramiro Condarco Morales, *Zárate: El temible Willca: Historia de la rebelión indígena de 1899* (La Paz, 1965). On race war, see, René Zavaleta Mercado, "El mundo del Temible Willka," en *Lo nacional-popular in Bolivia*, pp. 153–6; Marta Irurozqui, "La guerra de razas en Bolivia: La reinvención de una tradición," *Revista Andina* 21 (1993), p. 165 n. 2; idem, *La harmonía de las desigualdades: Elites y conflictos de poder en Bolivia, 1880–1920* (Madrid and Cusco 1994), p. 150; idem, "Discusión historiográfica sobre la rebelión indígena de 1899," in *La Rebelión Indígena de 1899*, Fascículo 7, *La Razón* (1999), pp. 15–16; E. Gabriela Kuenzli, "La evolución de la revolución liberal: de aymaras a incas ciudadanos," *Historia y Cultura* 28–9 (2003), pp. 253–4; Hylton, "El federalismo insurgente," pp. 101–2.

22 Our discussion here is based on Seemin Qayum's work on geography and internal colonialism in the first century of the republic. See "Creole Imaginings: Race, Space, and Gender in the Making of Republican Bolivia," pp. 184–218.

23 Erwin P. Greishaber, "La expansión de la hacienda en el departamento de La Paz, Bolivia, 1850–1920: Una revisión cuantitativa," *Revista Andes* 2/3 (1990–1), p. 51. See also Silvia Rivera, "La expansión del latifundio en el altiplano boliviano: Elementos para la caracterización de una oligarquía regional," *Avances* 2 (1978), pp. 95–118.

24 For resistance to these developments, see Gonzalo Flores, "Levantamientos campesinos durante el período Liberal," in Dandler and Torrico, eds, *Bolivia: La fuerza histórica del campesinado* (La Paz, 1987), pp. 121–32.

25 Ticona and Condori Chura, *El escribano de los caciques apoderados/Kasikinakan purirarkunakan quillqiripa*, p. 60.

26 Bautista Saavedra, *El ayllu (segunda parte, Proceso Mohoza)* (La Paz, 1995).

27 Roberto Choque and Esteban Ticona, *Jesús de Machaqa: Sublevación y masacre de 1921* (La Paz, 1996), Anexo 2, pp. 187–8.

28 Ibid., pp. 37–82.

Chapter 5

1 Archivo General de la Nación (AGN), Sucre, "Sublevación Indigenal" (1927), vol. 2, fols 14–15.

2 Quoted in Guillermo Lora, *Historia del movimiento obrero boliviano*, vol. 2 (La Paz, 1970), p.25.

3 Much of the following draws from Forrest Hylton, "Tierra común: Caciques, artesanos e intelectuales radicales y la rebelión de Chayanta," in Forrest Hylton, et al., *Ya es otro tiempo el presente*, pp.135–98.

4 Sergio Serulnikov, " 'Su ley y su justicia': Tomás Catari y la insurrección aymara de Chayanta, 1777–1780," in Charles Walker, ed., *Entre la retórica y la insurgencia: Las ideas y los movimientos sociales en los Andes, siglo XVIII* (Cuzco, 1996); published in English as idem, "Disputed Images of Colonialism: Spanish Rule and Indian Subversion in Northern Potosí, 1777–1780," *Hispanic American Historical Review* 76:2 (1996), pp.189–226.

5 Ticona and Condori Chura, op. cit., p.64.

6 For example, in order to fund railroads, a central bank, and other public works projects, Siles's predecessor Saavedra negotiated a $33,000,000 "Nicolaus" loan, the terms of which dictated that the United States exercise direct control over Bolivian taxation. Herbert Klein, *Bolivia: Evolution of a Multiethnic Society* (Oxford, 1982), p.79; idem, *Parties and Political Change: 1880–1952* (Chicago, 1969), pp.103–4.

7 Klein, *Bolivia*, p.152. The bulk of the dispossession occurred in the department of La Paz.

8 "Sublevación Indigenal," vol. 2, fol. 96.

9 James Dunkerley, "The Origins of the Bolivian Revolution in the Twentieth Century: Some Reflections," in Grindle and Domingo, eds, *Proclaiming Revolution*, pp.144–5.

10 René Arze Aguirre, *Guerra y conflictos sociales: El caso rural boliviano durante la campaña del Chaco* (La Paz, 1987), p.86.

11 Ibid., pp.85–109. The land takeovers occurred in Guaqui, Tiwanaku, Pucarani, Achacachi, Sicasica, Ayo Ayo, Tiquina, Ambaná, Puerto Acosta, and Coroico.

12 Carlos Mamani, *Taraqu*, pp.134–53.

13 Klein, *Parties and Political Change*; Malloy, *Incomplete Revolution*.

14 Marta Irurozqui, "Partidos Políticos y Golpe de Estado en Bolivia: La Política Nacional-Popular de Bautista Saavedra, 1921–1925," *Revista de Indias*, vol. LIV, no. 200 (1994), pp. 137–56. Hylton, "Tierra Común," p.144.

15 Ferran Gallego, "Los orígenes de la revolución nacional boliviana: El trienio del 'socialismo militar' (1936–39)," *Data* 3 (1992), pp.23–36.

Chapter 6

1 Roberto Choque Canqui, "Las rebeliones indígenas de la post-guerra del Chaco: Reivindicaciones durante la prerevolución," in ibid., pp. 37–54. Ramón Conde Mamani, "La lucha por la educación indígena, 1900–45," *Data* 5 (1993), pp. 85–96.

2 Quevedo was the son of a Quechua smallholder from Cochabamba's Valle Bajo. For the Congress and the 1946–7 rebellion, see Laura Gotkowitz, "Revisiting the Rural Roots of the Revolution," in Grindle and Domingo, eds, *Proclaiming Revolution*. For more on indigenous politics and the state in the 1930s and 1940s, see idem, *A Revolution for Our Rights: Indigenous Struggle for Land and Justice in Bolivia, 1880–1952* (Durham, NC, 2007).

3 Massacres occurred in Pucarani, Caquiaviri, Ayo Ayo, Laja, Yahani, Ayopaya, Topohoco, Tarabuco, Macha, and Chayanta. The last four had been key sites of insurgent mobilization in 1927. For the mobilization and repression in this period, see Silvia Rivera Cusicanqui, *"Oprimidos pero no vencidos": Luchas del campesinado aymara-quechwa, 1900–80*, 4th ed. (La Paz, 2003 [1983]), pp. 55–75; Jorge Dandler and Juan Torrico, "El Congreso Nacional Indígena y la rebelión campesina de Ayopaya (1947)," in Dandler and Torrico, eds, *Bolivia: La fuerza histórica del campesinado* (La Paz, 1987), pp. 136–200; Fernando Montes, *La máscara de piedra: Simbolismo y personalidad aymaras en la historia*, 2nd ed. (La Paz, 1999), pp. 346–50; Gotkowitz, "Revisiting the Rural Roots," p. 166; and idem, *A Revolution for Our Rights*.

4 Luis Antezana and Hugo Romero, *Historia de los sindicatos campesinos* (Le Paz, 1973), pp. 141–4. Miners would acquire a more direct influence over rural organizing after 1952. See Rivera, *Oprimidos*, pp. 84, 98–100, 102–9; and Steven Sándor John, "Permanent Revolution on the Altiplano: Bolivian Trotskyism, 1928–2005," Ph.D. Thesis, CUNY, 2005.

5 James Malloy, *The Incomplete Revolution* (Pittsburgh, PA, 1970), p. 188. Herbert Klein, *Parties and Political Change in Bolivia, 1880–1952* (Cambridge, 1969), pp. 383–402. Idem, *Bolivia: Evolution of a Multiethnic Society* (Oxford, 1982), p. 234.

6 Alan Knight, "The Domestic Dynamics of the Mexican and Bolivian Revolutions Compared," in Grindle and Domingo, eds, *Proclaiming Revolution*, pp. 55–6, 69.

7 Claudia Ranaboldo, *El camino perdido. Chinkasqa ñan armat thaki. Biografía del dirigente campesino kallawaya Antonio Alvarez Mamani* (La Paz, 1987), pp. 133–4, 143–7. The literature points to miners' roots in the growth of a landless class within Cochabamba's Quechua-speaking mestizo peasant culture, which led to waves of out-migration in the nineteenth and twentieth centuries. See Brooke Larson, *Cochabamba, 1550–1900: Colonialism and Agrarian Transformation in Bolivia* (Durham, NC, 1998); Gustavo Rodríguez Ostría, *Entre el socavón y el sindicato: Ensayos históricos sobre los trabajadores mineros, Siglos XIX–XX* (La Paz, 1991), pp. 57–145; Robert Smale, "Above and Below: Peasants and Miners in Oruro and Northern Potosí, 1899–1929," Ph.D. Thesis, University of Texas at Austin, 2005. The point to emphasize is that in spite of rural roots, mine workers' culture and communities became increasingly distinguished from peasant culture and communities, especially during the 1950s and '60s with the development of proletarian identity and struggle. For the roots of the split in northern Potosí, see Olivia Harris and Xavier Albó, *Montoneras y guardatojos en el norte de Potosí* (La Paz, 1986 [1974]). For a proletarian view, see Filemón Escobar, *La mina vista desde el guardatojo* (La Paz, 1986).

8 James Dunkerley, "The Origins of the Bolivian Revolution in the Twentieth Century: Some Reflections," in Grindle and Domingo, eds, *Proclaiming Revolution*, pp. 141–2, 150. Knight, "The Domestic Dynamics," in ibid., pp. 61, 86. See also Magdalena Cajías, "Los mineros en la revolución nacional: La identidad minera y su accionar sindical y político," *Data* 3 (1992), pp. 55–72. For the memories of a mid-century witness to the political culture of miners, see Sinclair Thomson and Seemin Qayum, "'Ahora que lo pienso, cincuenta años después . . .': Adolfo Gilly recuerda a mitos, mineros y la revolución en Bolivia," *Historias* 6 (La Paz, 2003), pp. 239–58.

9 James Dunkerley, *Rebellion in the Veins: Political Struggle in Bolivia, 1952–1982* (London, 1984), p. 20.

10 Jorge Dandler, "Campesinado y reforma agraria en Cochabamba (1952–53): Dinámica de un movimiento campesino en Bolivia," in Dandler and Torrico, eds, *Bolivia*, pp. 203–39.

11 Herbert Klein, "Social Change in Bolivia since 1952," in Grindle and Domingo, eds, *Proclaiming Revolution*, pp. 232–7.

12 Jorge Dandler, *El sindicalismo campesino en Bolivia: Los cambios estructurales en Ucureña* (La Paz, 1983, re-edition).

13 Cited in Sándor John, "Permanent Revolution on the Altiplano," p. 215.

14 Cited in Lynch, *Spanish American Revolutions*, p. 277.

15 The foremost MNR historical narrative is Carlos Montenegro's *Nacionalismo y coloniaje* (La Paz, 1954). See also Sinclair Thomson, "Revolutionary memory," in Grindle and Domingo, eds, *Proclaiming Revolution.*

16 Knight, "Domestic Dynamics," in ibid., p. 76. Siles Zuazo was the first president to subsidize the agro-industrial development of the east on a large scale: 57.7 percent of all credits from the Agrarian Bank went to Santa Cruz, where sugar and rice production soared. In important respects, he prefigured political-economic developments in the 1970s.

17 William Stokes, "The Foreign Aid Program in Bolivia," *The Western Political Quarterly* 15: 3, (1962), pp. 28–30.

18 Dunkerley, "The Origins," in Grindle and Domingo, eds, *Proclaiming Revolution*, p. 158.

Chapter 7

1 René Zavaleta Mercado, *Clases sociales y conocimiento* (La Paz, 1988), pp. 30, 34, 39, 135.

2 The contrast with Colombia, where trade unionism was weak and guerrilla insurgency became the preferred means of opposition from the 1960s through the mid-1980s, could hardly be sharper. See Forrest Hylton, "An Evil Hour: Colombia in Historical Context," *New Left Review* 23 (November–December 2003), pp. 51–93; and Rodrigo Uprimny Yepes, "Violence, Power, and Collective Action: A Comparison between Bolivia and Colombia," in Charles Bergquist et al., eds, *Violence in Colombia, 1990–2000: Waging War and Negotiating Peace* (Wilmington, DE, 2001), pp. 39–52.

3 René Zavaleta Mercado, "Bolivian Military Nationalism and People's Assembly," *New Left Review* 73 (May–June 1971), pp. 63–82, translated from idem, *El poder dual en América Latina* (Mexico, 1974). See also, Dunkerley, *Rebellion*, p. 192–3.

4 For the political life of Banzer, see Martín Sivak, *El dictador elegido: Biografía no autorizada de Hugo Banzer Suárez* (La Paz, 2001).

5 Fausto Reinaga, *La revolución India* (La Paz, 1969).

6 For a translation of the "Manifesto of Tiwanaku" in English, see Roger Moody, ed., *The Indigenous Voice: Visions and Realities*, 2nd ed. (Utrecht, 1988), pp. 476–83.

7 Silvia Rivera Cusicanqui, *"Oprimidos pero no vencidos": Luchas del campesinado aymara-quechwa, 1900–80*, 4th ed. (La Paz, 2003[1983]), pp. 152–3; Diego Pacheco, *El indianismo y los indios contemporáneos en Bolivia* (La Paz, 1992). For an account by a leading participant in *indianista* politics, see Luciano Tapia (Lusiku Quispi Mamani), *Ukhamawa jakawisaxa (Así es nuestra vida): Autobiografía de un aymara* (La Paz, 1995), pp. 329–73.

8 René Bascopé Aspiazu, *La veta blanca: Coca y cocaína en Bolivia* (La Paz, 1982), pp. 90–3.

9 For Plan Condor, see John Dinges, *The Condor Years: How General Pinochet and His Allies Brought Terror to Three Continents* (New York, 2005).

10 Perhaps the lack of urban guerrilla forces like those prominent in opposition politics in the Southern Cone helped limit the scope of state terror under Banzer. As compared to Chile and Uruguay after 1973 or Argentina after 1976, the Banzer regime does not stand out for its violence. Dunkerley, *Rebellion*, p. 202.

11 Rivera, *Oprimidos*, pp. 124–62. See also, Javier Hurtado, *El katarismo* (La Paz, 1986); Xavier Albó, "From MNRistas to Kataristas to Katari," in Steve Stern, ed., *Resistance, Rebellion, and Consciousness in the Andean Peasant World, 18th to 20th Centuries* (Madison, WI, 1987).

12 Natusch Busch was from the politically conservative, cattle-ranching department of Beni.

13 Zavaleta *Las masas en noviembre.*

14 Cited in Dunkerley, *Rebellion*, p. 322. On the development of cocaine production, its intimate relationship with the successive military dictatorships from Banzer to García Meza, and its fusion with capital from government-subsidized lowland agribusiness, see Bascopé, *La veta blanca*. By 1983, in Santa Cruz there were 500 airstrips, and in Beni, 3,000. Narco-aviators plied the route to Leticia, Colombia, where paste base was refined into cocaine—the first step in its complicated passage to Florida.

Chapter 8

1 Jeffrey Sachs, "The Bolivian Hyperinflation and Stabilization," *American Economic Review* 77:2 (1987), pp. 279–83.

2 Latin America Bureau, *The Great Tin Crash: Bolivia and the World Tin Market* (London, 1987). *NACLA Report on the Americas*, "Bolivia: The Poverty of Progress," 25:1 (1991), pp. 12, 18.

3 Most of the "relocated" miners settled in the cities of El Alto and Cochabamba, or the agricultural valley and lowland regions of La Paz, the Chapare, and Santa Cruz. They brought with them the traditions of radical trade unionism and community activism forged in mining communities over the previous half-century and swelled the ranks of popular neighborhood and colonizers' organizations.

4 James Painter, *Bolivia and Coca: A Study in Dependency* (Boulder, CO, 1994).

5 Jaime Iturri Salmón, *EGTK: La guerrilla aymara en Bolivia* (La Paz, 1992). Idem and Raquel Gutiérrez, *Entre hermanos: Porque queremos seguir siendo rebeldes, es necesaria la subversión de la subversión* (La Paz, 1995).

6 While the state has been unable to dismantle the *cocalero* movement, coca growers have been subject to more frequent detention, torture, and killing than any other social or political sector in recent Bolivian history, and are most frequently accused of having "narco-terrorist" links.

7 The US would employ a similar strategy to control Cesar Gaviria's successor in Colombia, Ernesto Samper (1994–8). Because he had financed his campaign with help from the Cali cartel, Samper could not but deepen the neoliberal reforms dictated by Gaviria in accordance with the "Washington Consensus." Forrest Hylton, "An Evil Hour: Colombia in Historical Context," *New Left Review* 23 (November–December 2003).

8 Xavier Albó, "And from Kataristas to MNRistas? The Surprising and Bold Alliance between Aymaras and Neoliberals," in Donna Van Cott, ed., *Indigenous Peoples and Democracy in Latin America* (New York, 1994). Pamela Calla and Susan Paulson, "Gender and Ethnicity in Bolivian Politics: Transformation or Paternalism?" *Journal of Latin American Anthropology* 5:2 (2000), pp. 112–49. Bret Gustafson, "Paradoxes of Liberal Indigenism: Indigenous Movements, State Process, and Intercultural Reform in Bolivia," in David Maybury Lewis, ed., *Identities in Conflict: Indigenous Peoples in Latin American States* (Cambridge, MA, 2002).

9 Benjamin Kohl, "Privatization Bolivian Style: A Cautionary Tale," *International Journal of Urban and Regional Research* 28: 4 (2004), pp. 893–908.

10 Sánchez de Lozada's own investments, primarily in the private mining sector, were the exception to the rule. By the time he left office, Sánchez de Lozada had an estimated personal fortune of more than $200 million. Only his brother was richer. See Andrés Soliz Rada, *La fortuna del presidente* (2nd ed., La Paz, 2004).

11 According to Transparency International, Bolivia was ranked as one of the most corrupt countries in the world under Banzer's civilian government.

Note on sources, Chapters 9–11

Our account in Chapters 9, 10, and 11 is drawn from personal observation in Bolivia and an array of sources. Bolivian periodical sources include: *El Diario, El Juguete Rabioso, La Prensa, La Razón, Pulso*. Bolivian radio stations include: Radio Erbol, Radio Fides, Radio Pachamama, Radio Wayna Tambo. Bolivian television stations include: PAT, Canal 11, RTP. On-line news services include: Bolpress, Econoticias. Some of this is based on previous articles by Forrest Hylton, available at: www.counterpunch.org. See also our articles "The Chequered Rainbow," *New Left Review* 35 (September–October 2005), pp. 40–64; and "Insurgent Bolivia," *NACLA Report on the Americas* 38:3 (2004), updated in Teo Ballvé and Vijay Prashad, eds, *Dispatches from Latin America: On the Frontlines Against Neoliberalism* (Cambridge, MA, 2006).

Chapter 9

1 Benjamin Kohl, "Privatization Bolivian Style," pp. 901–4.
2 *Econoticias*, www.econoticias.com (8 December 2003); *The Economist*, 21 April 2005.
3 Tom Lewis and Oscar Olivera, eds, *Cochabamba!*, p. 38.
4 See Jim Schultz, "Bolivia: The Water War Widens," *NACLA Report on the Americas* (January–February 2003), pp. 34–7.
5 Oscar Olivera spoke of the experience to crowds gathered to shut down Washington, DC, on 19–20 April, 2000.
6 The Aymara term *mallku* means condor, and refers to a political-spiritual leadership role of pre-conquest origin.
7 *Q'ara*, meaning naked or bald, refers to someone who lives parasitically off the community through exploitation, and is frequently used as a synonym for "whites," or mestizos, creoles, and foreigners as distinguished from Indians. For a historically grounded chronicle of Aymara mobilization in 2000–1, see Magdalena Cajías de la Vega, "Rebelión y negociación en el mundo aymara boliviano," in Eric Lair and Gonzalo Sánchez, eds, *Violencias y estrategias colectivas en la región andina* (Bogotá, 2004), pp. 485–516.
8 In addition to rejecting a series of neoliberal measures on land, water, mining, forests, and local government, the CSUTCB did demand a halt to forced eradication in the Yungas, where coca leaves for the internal market of coca leaf chewers have traditionally been grown.
9 Herbert Klein, "Social Change in Bolivia since 1952," in Grindle and Domingo, eds, *Proclaiming Revolution*, pp. 244–6. Alvaro García Linera, "Impedir la restauración neoliberal: La opción boliviana," *Le Monde Diplomatique*, January 2003 (Bolivia), p. 5.
10 Máximo Quisbert, *FEJUVE El Alto, 1990–1998: Dilemas del clientelismo colectivo en un mercado político en expansión* (La Paz, 2003), pp. 21–30. Since land occupation, as well as building and construction activity, in El Alto are largely informal, extra-legal, and self-organized, and the rate of migration is high, most figures are in fact estimates of greater or lesser precision. The same is true of census data.
11 Gómez, *El Alto de pie*, pp. 14, 18.
12 Miguel Pinto, comp., *Lecciones del levantamiento popular del 12 y 13 de Febrero* (La Paz, 2003).

Chapter 10

1 For an analysis of women's leadership and participation in the new revolutionary cycle, see Denise Y. Arnold and Alison Spedding, *Mujeres en los movimientos sociales en Bolivia, 2000–2003* (La Paz, 2005).
2 On the conflicted relation between self-organized *cooperativistas* and state-employed mine-workers, see Magdalena Cajías de la Vega, "Articulaciones ideológicos y culturales en los movimientos sociales: El poder de la memoria," *Barataria*, 1:1 (2004), 28. In analyzing political articulation in 2003 in terms of the historical memory of miners, indigenous peasants, and coca growers, Cajías uses an analytical lens similar to ours.
3 Gómez, *El Alto de pie*, p.137.
4 Pablo Mamani, "Microgobiernos barriales en El Alto," *Barataria* 1:1 (October–December 2004), pp.29–32. Idem, *El rugir de las multitudes: La fuerza de los levantamientos indígenas en Bolivia/Qollasuyu* (La Paz, 2004).

Chapter 11

1 The concession for water and sewage had been granted in 1997 as a condition for World Bank loans, and initial hook-ups cost $445. Many of the *alteños* who had connections were priced out of the market by rising utilities bills.

Chapter 12

1 Quoted in Juan Forero, "Coca Advocate Wins Election for President in Bolivia," *New York Times*, 19 July 2005.

2 Quoted in Alex Contreras, "La revolución democrática boliviana: Una vuelta al mundo junto al primer Presidente Indígena," *Servicio Informativo Alai-Amlatina*, 13 January 2006; *La Prensa*, 14 May 2006.

3 Stefanoni and do Alto, *Evo Morales: De la coca al palacio* (La Paz, 2006), pp. 53–5.

4 See *Crítica de la nación y la nación crítica* (La Paz, 1989), and *De demonios escondidos y momentos de revolución* (La Paz, 1991). While in prison he wrote *Forma valor y forma comunidad en los procesos de trabajo* (La Paz, 1995).

5 See also *Espacio social y estructuras simbólicas: Clase, dominación simbólica y etnicidad en la obra de Pierre Bourdieu* (La Paz, 1999) and *Estado multinacional* (La Paz, 2005).

6 Morales quoted in José Pinto and Antonio Solares, *Alai-Amlatina*, 19 December 2005. Alvaro García Linera, "El evismo: Retorno de lo nacional-popular," *El Juguete Rabioso*, 2 March–5 April, 2006.

7 Forrest Hylton, "Landslide in Bolivia," *New Left Review* 37 (January–February 2006), p. 70.

8 Stefanoni and do Alto, *Evo Morales*, p. 163. For the text of the decree, see Evo Morales Ayma, "Decreto 28701 de la nacionalización de los hidrocarburos," 1 May 2006: www.abi.bo

9 Lorgio Orellana Aillón, "Nacionalismo, populismo, y régimen de acumulación en Bolivia: Hacia una caracterización del régimen de Evo Morales," *Documentos de Coyuntura* 11, August 2006. James Petras, "Is Latin America Really Turning Left?" *CounterPunch*, 3–4 June 2006: www.counterpunch.org. Jeffery R. Webber, "The First 100 Days of Evo Morales: Image and Reality in Bolivia," *Against the Current* vol. XXI: 3 (July–August 2006), pp. 11–20. CEDLA, "Legitimando el orden neoliberal: 100 días de gobierno de Evo Morales," *Documentos de Coyuntura* 12, August 2006.

10 Stefanoni and do Alto, *Evo Morales*, p. 165.

11 Gretchen Gordon, "President Evo Morales' Gas and Oil 'Nationalization' Decree," June 2006, Democracy Center—Bolivia Briefing Series: www.democracycenter.org. Pablo Stefanoni and Walter Chávez, "Bolivia en revolución," *Le Monde Diplomatique* (Colombia), June 2006. Petrobras controlled close to half of total production, and Repsol just over one fifth.

12 Alan Clandenning, "Bolivian Gas Conflict Cooks as Election Nears," *The Miami Herald.com*, 22 September 2006.

13 Gretchen Gordon, "Waiting for Nationalization," 17 October 2006: news.nacla.org.

14 Citations from Aaron Luoma, "Evo Morales' Gas and Oil 'Nationalization' Decree: A Review of the International Media Coverage," *Democracy Center—Bolivia Briefing Series*, June 2006: www.democracycenter.org. "Bolivia Stirs Fears of Energy Producer Power," *Reuters*, 2 May 2006; "Bolivia Plays Risky Game," *Business Week Online*, 3 May 2006; "Leaders Back Bolivia Gas Nationalization," *Associated Press*, 5 May 2006; "Bolivia Gas Plan Causes Rift in South America," *ABC News International*, 10 May 2006.

15 "Nationalization Fuels Fears about Evo Morales's Power," *Financial Times*, 2 May

2006. "Bolivia's President Plays Nationalist Card," *Miami Herald*, 3 May 2006. "Bolivian Gas Takeover Sets a Familiar Scene," *Washington Post*, 4 May 2006.

16 "New President Has Bolivia Marching to Chavez's Beat," *Wall Street Journal*, 25 May 2006. "Chirac Says Bolivia Oil, Gas Profits Should Help Poor," *Bloomberg News Service*, 24 May 2006.

17 Miguel Lora, "El plan tierra del gobierno respetará el latifundio productivo," *El Juguete Rabioso*, 14 May 2006. CEDLA, "Muy lejos de 'Revolución Agraria' " *Alerta Laboral*, 7 July 2006: www.cedla.com.

18 "García Linera prevé que solo un 10 o 20 percent de la Constitución será cambiado en la Asemblea Constituyente," 7 March 2006: www.bolpress.com.

19 See "Conclusiones de la Cumbre Social por la Asamblea Constituyente," 21 February 2006; "El MAS desecha la representación indígena y corporativa en la constituyente"; and "Constituyente: El MAS descarta las jurisdicciones étnicas por razones técnicas," 24 February 2006; Bernardo Ponce, "Cumbre Social por la Asamblea Constituyente: Indígenas fortalecen Pacto de Unidad," 26 February 2006; for the text of MAS's law, see "Ley Especial de Convocatoria a la Asamblea Constituyente," 17 March 2006: www.bolpress.com

20 Luis Tapia, "Subsuelo político," in Alvaro García et al., *Pluriverso: Teoría política boliviana* (La Paz, 2001).

21 For trenchant feminist critique, see Raquel Gutiérrez Aguilar and Dunia Mokrani Chávez, "Asamblea Constituyente: ¿Refundar o reformar el Estado?" 1 July 2006: www.ircamericas.org.

22 "Entrevista personal a Silvia Lazarte, Presidenta de la Asamblea Constituyente": www.agenciaacta.org.ar.

Conclusion

1 On the Andean cultural logic of complementary dualism and *tinku*, see Tristan Platt, "Mirrors and Maize: The Concept of *Yanantin* among the Macha of Bolivia," in John Murra, Nathan Wachtel, and Jacques Revel, eds, *Anthropological History of Andean Polities* (Cambridge, 1986), pp. 228–59; idem, *Los guerreros de Cristo* (La Paz, 1996), pp. 68–75, 82–3; Thérèse Bouysse-Cassagne and Olivia Harris, "Pacha: En torno al pensamiento ayamara," in Bouysse-Cassagne et al., *Tres reflexiones sobre el pensamiento aymara* (La Paz, 1987), pp. 29–31; Verónica Cereceda, "Aproximaciones a una estética andina: De la belleza al *tinku*, in ibid., pp. 211–12.

2 See chapter 4, note 11.

3 Walter Benjamin, "Theses on the Philosophy of History," in Benjamin, *Illuminations* (New York, 1969), pp. 254–8 (emphasis in the original).

4 Grupo Los Cronistas y Mónica Navia, *Y todo comenzó de nuevo. Memorias de octubre* (La Paz, 2004), p. 87.

5 Ibid., p. 179.

6 Ibid., pp. 46–7.

7 Ibid., pp. 262, 264.

8 Lina Britto, Lucila Choque, Forrest Hylton, and Colectivo de Mujeres Alteñas, *La guerra del gas contada desde la mujeres: Altupata warminakan sartasitapa lup'iwipampi wali ch'amampi* (La Paz, 2005), pp. 69, 75.

Acronyms

ADEPA—Cotton Producers' Association
ADN—Nationalist Democratic Action
AP—Popular Assembly
CNTC—National Peasant Workers' Confederation
COB—Bolivian Workers' Central
COD—Departmental Workers' Central
COR—Regional Workers' Central
COMIBOL—Bolivian Mining Corporation
CONDEPA—Consciousness of the Fatherland
CSUTCB—Trade Union Confederation of Bolivian Peasant Workers
EGTK—Tupac Katari Guerrilla Army
ELN—National Liberation Army
FEJUVE—Federation of Neighborhood Juntas
FOS—Workers' Trade Union Federation
FSB—Bolivian Socialist Phalange
FSTMB—Trade Union Federation of Bolivian Mine Workers
FTAA—Free Trade of the Americas Agreement
MAS—Movement Toward Socialism
MIP—Pachakuti Indigenous Movement
MIR—Revolutionary Left Movement
MITKA—Tupac Katari Revolutionary Indian Movement
MNR—National Revolutionary Movement
MNR-I—Nationalist Revolutionary Movement of the Left
MRTKL—Tupac Katari Revolutionary Movement of Liberation
MST—Landless Peasants' Movement
NFR—New Republican Force
PCB—Bolivian Communist Party
PCML—Marxist-Leninist Communist Party
PIR—Revolutionary Left Party
PODEMOS—Social Democratic Power
POR—Revolutionary Workers' Party
PS-1—Socialist Party-1
RADEPA—Patriotic Reason Party
UCS—Union of Civic Solidarity
UDP—Democratic Popular Unity
UPEA—Public University of El Alto
YPFB—Bolivian State Petroleum Company

Index